Volume 1

PROPHETIC BUILDING
(A NIGHTMARE OR VISION)
AN INSIGHT INTO THE BUILDING DILEMMAS

A PRACTICAL GUIDE for BUILDING

A PRACTICAL GUIDE
for BUILDING

©

Calvin C. Barlow, Jr., Author
905 South Douglas Avenue
Nashville, Tennessee 37204
Phone 615-383-7807
Email: barlow5561@bellsouth.net

ISBN 0-9764174-1-3
Published by Relevant Publishing, Inc.
2275 Murfreesboro Road, Suite 100
Nashville, TN 37217
615/366-3211

Edited and Proofread independently by
Mrs. Joan Yarborough

Printed in the United States of America.
All rights reserved under International Copyright Law.
Contents and/or cover may not be reproduced in whole or in part in any form without the express written consent of the Author.

Table of Contents

Acknowledgements

Foreword

Introduction

Chapter One	Why Should We Build?	8
Chapter Two	What Should We Consider?	14
Chapter Three	How Much Money Can We Borrow?	24
Chapter Four	The Architect	26
Chapter Five	The Middle Passage	42
Chapter Six	The General Contractor	47
Chapter Seven	Finding the Right Contractor	53
Chapter Eight	Construction Contracts	72
Chapter Nine	The Building Project and Church Members	77
Chapter Ten	Building Your Vision	81
Chapter Eleven	Scheduled Values & Payment Requests	87
Chapter Twelve	Home Improvement Companies	106
Appendix 1:	A Glossary of Terms	110
Appendix 2:	Funding Possibilities	118
Appendix 3:	States' Web Pages	121

Acknowledgements

Prophetic Building (A Nightmare or Vision) is my testimony of what God can do in the midst of a storm. As you read, know that God's blessings in the storm out-lives the storm. Sometimes, it is difficult to see God in the midst of hurt, disappointment, and failure of expectations. As a believer in Christ, I can assure you that what Satan does for evil, God can use for good. I have always wanted to publish. If I had not suffered a disappointed building initiative, I know in my heart that this book would not have lived. God used this experience to strengthen my faith and to motivate my writing gift. Thanks and Glory to the name above all names, Jesus Christ.

Finally, I give a shout out to Andre Johnson, Esquire, for encouraging me and for reading my manuscript; to Mrs. Tiffany Johnson for proofreading my initial manuscript; to my wife, Rutha, who has stood by me for thirty-two years as an encourager and supported me to publish this work. Best wishes to Mrs. Joan Yarborough for helping me to edit and proofread my manuscript for print.

Foreword

Bishop Joseph Warren Walker, III
Pastor, Mount Zion Baptist Church
Nashville, Tennessee

Every now and then a book comes along that offers practical solutions to pastors, churches, and individuals who engage in building projects. Pastor Barlow contribution to this subject is incredible. As a pastor who has engaged in several building campaigns, I am personally aware of the challenges associated with mammoth tasks such as these. I am convinced that this is a must read for any leader serious about kingdom expansion in a spirit of excellence.

Pastor Barlow has brought years of wisdom as well as a host of guiding principles that can equip pastors and individuals toward the completion of any building campaign. Often, we approach these projects in the dark and make unnecessary mistakes due to a lack of information. The Bible says that we are "destroyed for a lack of knowledge." Knowledge is the key that eliminates many stumblingblocks.

Often, we are bombarded with theoretical insights that leave us practically deficient. I am so thankful that God spoke to Pastor Barlow in this area, because he clearly understands the need for practicality. Pastors and leaders, I encourage you to glean from the wealth of knowledge in this book. From a pastor's heart, this book is a powerful resource for you and your people. Let it bless you as it has blessed me.

For His Glory,
Bishop Joseph W. Walker, III

Introduction

"Unless the Lord builds the house those that labor; labor in vain"
Psalms 127:1 HCSB

The practical interpretation of God's word is broad. For persons who believe that the word of God offers guidance in every pursuit of life, God's word is not limited or locked in a historical epoch. When searching for a present or futuristic objective, one should always think outside of the box. For me, this verse can be interpreted to say, "Unless Godly wisdom and knowledge is used to build, your labor will cause you some sleepless nights."

This book comes out of my personal experience and research and from others who have shared with me the joy and pains of building. A word of caution: building **solely** on passion and zeal is damnation waiting to happen.

This book is not intended as a replacement for certified and professional assistance. It is the author's intent to provide a guide that will aid in the building process. The contents of the book are not based upon the creative imagination of the author but come out of research and having gone through a bad experience. It is the author's desire to spare others from un-necessary grief by sharing a retrospective view of the building process from thought, concept and to completion.

The book is styled as a workbook. Hopefully, those who teach will find "Prophetic Building (A Nightmare or Vision)" to be another tool for classroom instructions. Even though the book is written with religious institutions in mind, it can be used for any building project.

Finally, if you are a pastor, I recommend that you appoint a person to be responsible for the day-to-day activities of the building process. Building is like a woman giving birth, sometimes it is with ease and sometimes it is difficult." The problem is: you will not know until the process starts.

Chapter 1

WHY SHOULD WE BUILD?

> Except the Lord build the house, they labour in vain that build it: except the Lord keep the city, the watchman waketh but in vain. **(Psalms 127:1 KJV)**

There are perhaps as many justifications for building as there are buildings. Some churches build because other churches are building. However, most church projects come out of a perceived need. Often, the thought is first conceived in the mind of leadership. Some churches have shared leadership meaning that the pastor makes major decisions concerning church infrastructure with other leaders such as deacons and/or trustees. However, some building projects are conceived in the mind of the pastor and presented to the church. In some rare instances, the project is conceived by the pastor and shared with a selected group.

Unlike ancient times when God spoke to his prophets through dreams and visions, the visions of pastors need to be confirmed by the word of God and shared with other trusted and faithful leaders before implementing. *This is not saying that God does not speak to pastors but to say that God does not give us the whole.* The Bible is clear that no one person has all of the spiritual gifts or talents. The Bible names several characters that God spoke to but didn't give the whole picture. For this present time, you and I need gifts and talents of others to make our vision a reality of blessings.

I was talking with a pastor about building and he shared

with me that he was going to tear down his old sanctuary and build a new sanctuary. Knowing that his building was built to last for ages and that the basement of his church held historical values in the community, I asked; "do you intend to tear down the basement?" He stated, "I guess we could build on top of it." I asked; "Do you intend to make the church wider?" He stated, "I guess we could extent the church backward." Knowing that churches built their foundations for second floors in that era, I asked; "Do you intend to tear down the outer walls?" He stated, "I guess we won't know until we start the process." Now, the same preacher said to me earlier, "God had told him to tear the old building completely down."

The truth is: our vision is flawed. For most preachers, this might be a bitter pill that you don't want to swallow, but swallow it.

Not only is the preacher limited but all of God's people have limitations. Therefore, it is imperative that we seek the gifts and talents of others to carry out God's desire for kingdom building. Too often, God's people are intimidated by the fear of rejection. Don't allow your vision to become a nightmare because of the lack of qualified assistance.

Even though God called Moses and not Aaron, Moses was big enough to confess his limitations. Be a Moses and confess your limitations and seek others whom God has qualified to make your vision a reality.

Illustrationon 1

A random survey revealed that pastors built because of the following reasons.

      To modernize facilities

      Need for more space

      Current area declining in population

      Current area was not able to accommodate growth

      Moved from rented facilities

- To keep church current with its sister churches
- Future Codes Restrictions

Illustration 2

The idea to build came from the following sources.
- Pastor
- Pastors and Deacons
- Pastor and Trustees
- Pastor and Official Board
- Official Board or Building Committee
- Members

Illustration 3

> Noah, build me a boat! Man, I got several people and a few animals I want to save.

> God, I know that you are God but it has not rained since we been here. I know that you know all things but I thought I would remind you. We are not even close to a good creek!

> Noah, obey me and build the boat. Yes, Lord!

Even though needs precede the vision; sometimes messages are beyond human reasoning. Moses knew that the Israelites were in captivity but Noah had no knowledge of a flood.

If asked to build a mega church in a run-down community, what would you do?

Building needs to be based upon God's word, especially if it is to be blessed by God.

Illustration 4

> Genesis 11:4 (KJV)
>
> And they said, Go to, let us build us a city and a tower, whose top may reach unto heaven; and let us make us a name, lest we be scattered abroad upon the face of the whole earth.
>
> Genesis 11:8 (KJV)
>
> So the Lord scattered them abroad from thence upon the face of all the earth: and they left off to build the city.

A building project that seeks to glorify man is a pain not realized.

> Exodus 20:25 (KJV)
> And if thou wilt make me an altar of stone, thou shalt not build it of hewn stone: for if thou lift up thy tool upon it, thou hast polluted it.
>
> Zeph. 1:13 (KJV)
> Therefore their goods shall become booty, and their houses desolation: they shall also build houses, but not inhabit them; and they shall plant vineyards, but not drink the wine thereof.

No building project should be an undertaking with the notion of exclusion for the sake of building. In other words, if you cannot communicate need for the fear of rejection, perhaps the need does not exist. The project has to be God's project from conception to completion. Now, if the project is truly God's project then he has the responsibility to see that every nail and hammer is provided.

Because the actual building process cannot be pre-determined, it is best to have a team with a captain sailing the seas of uncertainty. Few building projects are smooth sailing. Do not be afraid to share your vision with others who may not support it. Often needed information comes from those who disagreed. In other words, sometimes God allows an adversary to have the missing link to the puzzle.

Finally, do not be afraid to go forth. Sometimes money may not be in the bank account. God will show you where it is. Sometimes money might be in the bank account but faith is bankrupted. God will show you how to stir up faith. Make sure that your dependency is in God from start to finish. Remember! A successful building project does not take form in a day.

Chapter One

Questions for Discussion

1. Why are we building?
   _____
   _____

2. Has the vision been communicated?
   _____
   _____

3. Have others agreed with the need?
   _____
   _____

4. Do I or we have a fear for not sharing the vision?
   _____
   _____

5. Whom will the project glorify?

_____
_____

6. Does human desire to build equal God's desire?
_____
_____

7. Does desire to build fulfill needs or satisfy a trend?
_____
_____

8. If we do not build, what will be the results?
_____
_____

9. Are we spiritually prepared to build?
_____
_____

10. Should we need to borrow funds, are records in order?
_____
_____

11. Do we have on hand adequate emergency funds?
_____
_____

12. Have we truly invited God to be an active participant?
_____
_____

Chapter 2

What Should We Consider?

Often, there is a temptation to say, "we will cross that bridge when we get there." Building is not a go-alone project but a planned initiative. First, you need to consider who will be the captain of the team. Second, determine who will be responsible for overseeing the project each day. This person does not need to be a full time person but a person that will be able to visit the project at least three times a day. This person should have the sole interest of the owner at heart and should have some knowledge of the construction trade.

The team should be assigned to gather information that will aid the building process:

1. What type of funding is available?
2. What type of building material is being considered for framing?
3. What professional services will be needed?
4. What is the condition of the soil to be built upon?
5. What environmental conditions need to be considered?
6. According to the planning commissioner, what are zoning and codes requirements for the proposed project?
7. Does the neighborhood have neighborhood associa-

tions and what is the councilman's position regarding the proposed project?

8. How will the proposed project impact parking requirements?

9. Does proposed project meet current needs without creating other uncontrollable problems?

10. How will materials be purchased?

The purpose of gathering this information allows you, the owner, to have more control of the building process. Furthermore, it increases your capacity to function as a knowledgeable owner. Do not allow this newly discovered knowledge to become a substitute for professional help.

Consideration Number One: Financing

Financing should be the second major consideration after a need is discovered. Having the right financing for your project can be the difference between headaches and joy. The right financing allows you to have a greater voice in moving your project ahead and it allows you to be in the driver's seat at the wheel. Regardless of the type of financing obtained, the owner has responsibilities. It is not the author's intent to describe in full details the type of financing available to owners but to state briefly types of financing that are available:

- Commercial Banks
- Church Bonds
- Venture Capital
- Church Mortgage Certificates
- Build-as-you-go financing
- Investment Capital

Detail descriptions of these types are in Appendix 2.

Consideration Number Two: Building Materials

There are primarily three types of materials used for framing: wood, steel and concrete blocks. Sometimes a combination of the three is used to complete the finished product. The decision to use any of the primary materials is usually based upon cost, type of project, appearance, and weight conditions of the project. Wood may be less in cost but it does not provide a fire rating protection and is subject to other defects. However, a good carpenter can usually make sure that it is protected from exposed weather conditions. The problem is that some builders will cut cost by not using the best grade of lumber. Concrete block buildings are preferred in some climates because concrete blocks retain the temperature better and provides good structure stability. Also, concrete blocks and steel are more durable materials. A concrete block building does require some extra prep for electrical and plumbing that may not be required for wood and steel. Rooms cannot be changed with ease when concrete blocks are used for internal walls. If you are in doubt about the best preferred construction type, a quick call to your local codes' administration office will be sufficient. Also, most general contractors will share this information. If you decide to add to the project in the future, the type of framing used determines future cost and possibilities.

Consideration Number Three:
Securing Professional Services

Do not make the mistake of not using qualified and certified professionals. The primary reason for seeking professional help is accountability. Licensed professionals usually have passed state boards and have a constant knowledge of their area of expertise. You should always ask questions and seek references before hiring contractors to start a project.

I personally recommend that you use the services of a real estate lawyer. When reviewing contracts to be signed or if a verbal agreement is used to perform services, you need the expertise of a lawyer. The upfront cost can save you unexpected and unseen expenses later. Second, if you intend to borrow money from a commercial bank, you need the advice of a certified accountant. However, depending upon current banking relationships and the size of the potential loan, an in-house person with accounting knowledge may be sufficient. I strongly recommend that you call several banks and get a copy of their requirements for securing a loan. Usually, banks require three or five years of previous history before making a loan. Third, you will need the services of a licensed architect. The architect will usually have on his staff a team comprised of licensed structure, mechanical, and electrical engineers. In some instances, you may require the service of a licensed surveyor. Fourth, you need a licensed and bonded general contractor. In no case should a contractor be used if he or she is not bonded. Having a performance bond guarantees the owner that funds will be available to complete the project should the contractor not finish it. Furthermore, contractors who are bonded are credit worthy and usually have sufficient cash flow to sustain a project. *Exception: when you personally know the contractor's work ethic and the cost of the job is twenty-five thousand dollars or less.* It is permissible to use a contractor who is not bonded. A word of caution: most banks will not consider making a loan if the contractor is not bonded and licensed. In no case should funds be paid to a contractor for work not in place. In a later chapter, I will share in details the steps in which contractors should be paid.

Finally, you will need a project manager. Most general contractors have a project manager and some banks will insist that you hire a consultant to protect their interest. For an additional cost, most architects will provide a project manager. However, the owner needs a person that has his interest at heart.

Consideration Number Four: Land Conditions

Not knowing the condition of the soil being built upon has the potential of ending your project before it is started. The size and weight of a building must be in proportion to its foundation. A foundation is strengthened by its footing. The width, depth and other requirements for the footing are determined by the type of soil. If the soil is rocky, blasting is usually required. Underground water requires other preventive methods. In some instances, cities have covered houses with dirt creating an unidentifiable landfill. Un-compacted soil usually require a concrete pile, in addition to extra footing. **The common problem is most plans will not show the condition of the soil unless requested.** Soil testing can be expensive. When a change occurs that is not on the plans, it is called a "change order". For example, if the contractor is not aware of the soil condition, he has the right to charge extra. This is called a "change order" and change orders can be expensive.

Consideration Number Five: Environmental Conditions

A church decided to purchase a farm that had several natural areas. Everybody agreed that this area was better than the other parcels. The other parcels had no trees, ponds, or creeks. The church had funds on hand to build, and an architect was hired to draw the plans. The job was bidden and a general contractor was hired. Two days after the general contractor started excavation a "stop work order" was issued by the state's environmental agencies. Why?

One neighbor knew that down-stream from the church, five-legged spotty frogs inhabited the water and they were on the endangered species list. Another neighbor knew that unusual birds lived in the woody areas that were also on the endangered species list. Before the church could continue their project, they had to agree to build a special bridge to get to the church. They had to set up special chemical barriers to prevent any potential constructional run-off into the creek which could have exposed it to possible environmental harm. Even though they had stamped plans and had been issued a permit to build, it would cost one hundred thousand dollars to go forward with the project. This story is fictional. However, two churches in Nashville, Tennessee faced environmental issues similar to these stories.

Therefore, be sure to contact historical and environmental agencies before hiring an architect to draw your plans.

Consideration Number Six: Zoning Requirements

Just because you have funds and land does not mean that you can build. Knowing what you can build is very important. There are several things that need to be considered:

What can be built on the property according to current

zoning?

What can be grandfathered?

What needs to be up-dated to meet new codes requirements?

What is the property offset: from street, highway, or other adjoined properties?

What safety issues must be considered and met in order to build?

How will the project impact current parking requirements?

Will the project impact current traffic flow and to what degree?

During the design phase, to whom will the architect report?

A good architect should have the answer to some of the above questions. However, the architect may not know or share with you things that would necessitate a "change order". A general contractor who is not familiar with the area may not be able to answer all of the above questions. Your best resources are codes administration's offices, your councilman or other city/state officials that understand zoning requirements such as: the local planning commission or state building codes department.

Consideration Number Seven: Associations

Most communities have neighborhood associations or some type of association that addresses new construction. If the project will require codes to make some exceptions for the church or homeowner, a variance will be required. It is best to involve your neighborhood association in this process.

First, decide which statutes govern the variance. Second, explain to the association what you are asking codes' officials to allow and seek the association's input. Be prepared to make minor changes to your project, initially. Having the association on your side can go a long way. However, if they oppose, be prepared for a good fight during the appeal process. At this point, it is crucial that you have your councilman and letters from other neighbors who support your project.

Just because you are an organization or homeowner who has lived in the neighborhood for a long time, is no guarantee that your neighbors will approve of your building project.

Therefore, it is suggested that you become a member of the association or associations. This could positively win over members of the association.

Consideration Number Eight: Parking

Parking is essential for commercial buildings, and in some instances; homeowners are restricted from parking as they wish. In the city of Nashville, Tennessee, Metro council passed a city ordinance that makes it illegal to park on grass or gravel. This means as a homeowner, you cannot park on your lawn. Many cities have ordinances that restrict parking on streets to conform to neighborhood growth and style. Therefore, it is imperative that parking be addressed and considered before designing a building. In some instances, you may not be able to build or may need to modify your project to meet local codes' requirements. In the city of Nashville, Tennessee, a local pastor shared with me that not having adequate parking prevented him from building a new edifice.

For example, churches depend upon the city to determine parking capacity as it relates to seating capacity of the sanctuary. The formula for determining the amount of parking space varies from city to city or area to area. Those who build in certain surrounding areas may not be subjected to the same formula as another area. Officials in zoning or the Fire Marshal's office should be able to answer these types of questions. If you are building a family life center that has activities that include non-members and scheduled hours, you will be subjected to additional parking requirements. If you plan to have a school in or near your facility, you may be subjected to additional parking requirements.

Consideration Number Nine: Domino Effect

Sometimes building creates a domino effect. Especially, if you intend to add to an existing structure or remodel an existing structure that requires you to pull a permit.

For example, you are a medium-size, non-profit organization. The organization has a small kitchen with a stove. The stove is a residential model with or without a hood. It is used to warm food for special gatherings and a breakfast ministry for the homeless. The stove does not meet existing codes' requirements. You are not in violation of the city ordinance because of a grandfathered clause. However, once you pull a new permit you lose your grandfathered status and you are subjected to a Fire Marshal's determination. Be sure to know all former and current codes requirements relating to existing equipment, wiring, plumbing and safety issues!

Increasing the square footage of an existing structure may subject the owner to current safety regulations. Codes' requirements for sprinkler and fire alarm systems, for most commercial buildings, are based upon the nature of business being conducted, square footage, height, and/or fire rating of building materials. These requirements are often a combination of each other. However, most churches fall into a category of square footage and fire rating of building materials. Therefore, if you increase your square footage over the calculated minimum formula, you will be subjected to up-grade your safety features.

Beware of the possible domino effect! It will add to the cost of your project. If the effect is known, the design can be modified.

Consideration Number Ten: Purchasing

The purchase method of materials can save or add cost to a building project. Most states require the contractors to add sales taxes to their bids. The only way to receive sales tax savings is for the organization to pay for all materials involved in the project. Most contractors will not have a problem with this method. Beware of a contractor that has a problem with an individual buying and paying for its materials. In some instances, these contractors will buy materials, bill the individual or organization and the owners will end up paying the vendors. If the individual or organization pays for all materials used in its project upfront, it minimizes the possibility of mechanic's liens against the property. Mechanic's liens usually show up at the end of the project or when a title search is performed.

Chapter Two
Questions for Discussion

1. Do we have a team leader for our committee?

2. To whom will the leader report?

3. Do we understand the things to be considered and why?

4. Which considerations are the most important for the project?

5. Which financing option will be used and why?

6. Are the financial records in order?

7. Why is the councilmember's involvement important?

8. Why is the neighborhood association's involvement important?

9. Why is soil type important?

10. Why should environmental and historical agencies be contacted?

11. Why should the owner purchase its materials?

12. Will the pursuit of the project create a domino effect and how?

Chapter 3

How Much Money Can We Borrow

The amount of funds required to build determines the size of your project. If you intend to borrow the funds, a lending institution will need to know the cost of the proposed building. To know the actual cost of a building project requires approved plans and a general contractor's bid price. The problem with this approach is: you are speculating.

Let say that you hire Jones Architectural Firm to draw plans for a huge state of art commercial kitchen, fancy restrooms with lockers and showers, huge classrooms and a suite of offices and he gives you a construction budget of one million dollars. You take your codes approved plans to the bank. They asked for records and in the process they determine that you can only borrow seven hundred thousand dollars ($700,000.00). You have just paid for some fancy paper with an official stamp! If the architect has to scale the plans down to achieve what you can afford, it will cost you additional funds. I personally know of a church that faced this problem.

I strongly suggest that you call several banks and asked to be pre-qualified for a loan. To determine how much you can borrow, take your monthly residual funds and multiply that number by 12. Then take the answer and multiply it by 30. Take this amount and multiply is by it by (.65 = (65%). This will provide an estimate of what you can afford. When banks ask how much you need to borrow, you will be able to verbalize a figure that did not cost you any out-of pocket expense.

The above formula is not scientific. It is a formula that I have developed from my years in real estate and banking experiences. In appendix 2, you will find a summary detail of most banks' requirements. However, to be safe my estimate is a low end figure and will hold up if your net income dollar amount is factual.

Example:

Average monthly funds after all bills are paid: $1,200.00

Monthly residual funds X 12 months = $14,400.00

$14,400 X 30 years = $432,000.00

$432,000.00 X .65 = $280,800.00

$280,800.00 = Potential Loan Amount

Using this method, the banks have tangible figures. The bank will take these figures and scrutinized your records to see if you qualify for more or less. Please keep in mind that most banks will ask for certified records such as: revenue statements and financial statements showing types of assets and liabilities. Therefore, if you don't have a CPA, you might need to employ one to satisfy the bank. You can save cost by hiring a CPA to provide you with the forms that will be needed to certify your records. The fewer discoveries involved: less your expenses will be. This cost cannot be circumvented unless the bank chooses to omit the requirements. Some banks will not require certified statements if you have an open account with them. Other banks with provide you with the forms to determine the legitimacy of your claim for funds.

Chapter 4

The Architect

Finding the right architect for your project is crucial. In 1968, Frank T. Greer, former band director of Tennessee State University, in Nashville, Tennessee said to me, two things are important when it comes to playing a composition, "how you start and how you end." In 1986, upon my call to pastor Second Missionary Baptist Church in Nashville, Tennessee, my father, Calvin Coolidge Barlow, Senior, said to me, "Start the way you want to end." The architect is the official start of your project! The way you start will be the way you end.

A good architect will protect your project from start to finish because his or her name is attached to the project. The architect takes your vision and concept and materializes it upon paper. He or she envisions how the finished product will look before it is finished. The architect knows how the facility will be used. Therefore, the right architect takes pride in your vision because it becomes his or her momentary reality as publisher of your vision.

The question is how do you find the right architect? Keep in mind just because one is licensed does not mean that he or she is the right architect for your project. Just because the architect has no complaints against him or her, according to the "Better Business Bureau", does not mean that he or she is the right architect. There is a procedure for finding the right architect. While organizations like the Better Business Bureau or state agencies are a good start, there are no foolproof means of finding the right architect. However, there are steps that can be taken to employ the right architect.

Illustration 5

FINDING THE RIGHT ARCHITECT

> Matthew 7:7 (KJV)
>
> Ask, and it shall be given you; seek, and ye shall find; knock, and it shall be opened unto you:
>
> Architects are like doctors some are general practitioners and others are specialists. To end up with the right architects, you have to ask and seek.

Illustration 6

Your problems determine your needs!

> Luke 14:28 (KJV)
>
> For which of you, intending to build a tower, sitteth not down first, and counteth the cost, whether he has sufficient to finish it?
>
> Do we have potential codes problems to be resolved?
>
> Do we have potential neighborhood opposition?
>
> Do we plan to add to an existing structure?
>
> If you answer "yes" to any of the above questions, you need a specialist.

Illustration 7

What determines an architect to be called a specialist?

> Ephesians 4:11-12 (KJV)
>
> And he gave some, apostles; and some, prophets; and some, evangelists; and some, pastors and teachers; [12] for the perfecting of the saints, for the work of the ministry, for the edifying of the body of Christ:
>
> Architectural abilities are not spiritual gifts but they are talents. Talents lend themselves to creativity in certain areas.
>
> Some architects are challenged to work with existing structures.
>
> **This is called renovation.**
>
> Some architects are challenged to solve problems.
>
> **This is called determination.**
>
> Some architects never give less than their best regardless of the size of the project.
>
> **This is called integrity.**
>
> Some architects seek to establish professional relationships.
>
> **This is called wisdom.**
>
> Some architects keep themselves up-to-date on all facets of the building industry.
>
> **This is called knowledge.**

Illustration 8

How do you find the right architect?

> Proverbs 22:1 (KJV)
>
> A good name is rather to be chosen than great riches, and loving favor rather than silver and gold.
>
> **Other Owners**
> **General Contractors**
> **Architectural Associations**
> **Yellow Pages**
> **A Letter of Inquiry**

Regardless of your initial discovery, you should use an investigative form letter before hiring an architect. We live in a world where the truth is often "disguised in sheep's clothing". Sometimes people speak favorably of persons because of personal gain. Sometimes people are blind because of personal relationship. Sometimes people have professional relationships. Using an investigative form letter will aid you in discovering the truth.

Illustration 9

A Sample Letter

Dear:

    Our organization is considering adding classrooms, restrooms and office space to our current structure. Our structure is a one-story brick-veneer building with a concrete floor, asphalt roof and has approximately 8500 square feet. It was built in 1975 and we have not updated the plumbing or electrical.

Your firm was recommended to us by _____ (or, your firm is being considered because of advertisement in the yellow pages). If you have an interest in our project, would you be so kind to forward to us the requested information:

How many years in business? _____

Are you a member of Better Business Bureau? _____

Is your license current? _____

Does your firm carry insurance that protects its clients? _____

Please provide the names, addresses and phone numbers of three general contractors that you have worked with in the last two years.

Please provide the names, addresses and phone numbers for the contact person of three projects that your firm designed within the last two years.

Thanks,

In your opening paragraph, try to be brief and descriptive of your project whether it is a family life center, sanctuary or new structure. If the location of the project is different from the mailing address, provide it in the letter.

Illustration 10

Contractor's References

Re: AAA Architectural Firm

Dear

AAA Architectural Firm listed your firm as being one of the firms it has worked with in the last two years. Please take a moment and complete the questionnaire. You may return it by fax or in the postage-paid envelope.

Do you have a design-building relationship with the above

firm? _____

Do you share office space with the above firm? _____

Does the above firm own an interest in your firm directly or indirectly? _____

In your opinion, does the above firm demonstrate a working knowledge of the building process beyond the design process? _____

Does the above firm demonstrate a working knowledge to accommodate necessary changes in the field? _____

Were change orders necessitated because of field inspectors? _____

If yes, note how many? _____

Do you look forward to working in the future with the above firm? _____

Illustration 11

Owner's Reference

Re: AAA Architectural Firm

Dear

AAA Architectural firm listed you as a recent client. Please take a moment and complete the questionnaire. You may return it by fax or in the postage-paid envelope.

Are you related to the architect directly or indirectly? _____

Are any persons of the firm a member of your organization? _____

Did you have any "charge orders" that cost you more money? _____

If yes, did the contractor place the error on the architect's plans? _____

Did architectural oversight of plans create a general contractor "change order"? _____

Did the architect do a good job supervising the general contractor? _____

Did the contractor provide conditional lien releases from vendors and subcontractors on each draw request? _____

Did the architect demand from the general contractor a list of all subcontractors for work to be done on the project and provided you the same? _____

Who chose or recommended the general contractor?

Thanks,

The Architect's Contractual Relationship

The architect is responsible to the owner and is to protect the owner. The architect is to assure the owner that the project is being built as approved by government agencies. The architect is to make sure that no funds are paid to the general contractor for work not in place. If materials are on the premises, only the cost of materials and completed work should be paid. Payments to contractor should not be released unless the contractor provides owner with conditional lien releases for the cost of materials from the vendors and subcontractors' labor and/or material costs; and the materials are for job specification only.

The architect should take responsibility for all subordinates that contribute to the plans. If the electrical engineer fails to calculate the right voltages, and it costs the owner additional funds, it is the architect's error and not the contractor's. If the engineer could have discovered it, the architect is liable for any additional cost. In other words, professionals cannot apply textbook theory to a project without investigation. They must visit each job and record the facts. Make sure your architect carries "error and omission insurance". The project needs to be insured for the total cost of the project and not the fee charged to draw the plans. Faulty design is covered under the architect's insurance. For example, if it costs one million dollars to build your building and the plans cost was fifty thousand dollars, your maximum protection would only be fifty thousand dollars if you chose the later. To reduce the architect's potential liabilities, sometimes a fee charged protection plan is offered to a client for a reduction of design cost.

Make sure that the architect gives you a contract for the services to be provided. Do not sign the contract without your lawyer's advice. A word of caution: architects have ways of passing their responsibilities to other people's discovery. Therefore, you need to amend the contract to deal with discoveries.

Example: <u>The plans note the demolition of a wall but the architect uses a symbol that indicates drywall but it is actually a concrete wall. The contractor writes a "change order" for more funds because the bid was for drywall. Who is liable for the additional cost: the owner, contractor or architect? Unless, your contract with the architect addresses ambiguous, wrong or not sufficient information, the owner will usually end-up bearing the cost.</u>

<u>You intend to put an elevator in your building and the architect provides you with code-approved plans but on the date the elevator is to be installed, the elevator company refuses to install it. The elevator falls under a state code that addresses the depth of the pit and the structure of the weight-bearing wall. In order to comply, the walls and current pit need to be demolished. Who will pay for this additional cost? Your contract with the architects needs to address compliance with all agencies. There are too many discoveries that may happen to address them sufficiently; Therefore, I strongly suggest using a real estate or construction attorney who is familiar with the building "woes".</u>

Discovery is defined as the revelation of conditions that impose a greater financial burden upon an obligated person after a fact. In other words, a contractor bids to tear down a wall. While tearing down the wall, he had to stop because electrical wires were exposed within the wall. The contractor's discovery will cost him more money to tear down the wall. But who is obligated to pay for it, the contractor, architect or owner? Therefore, it is very important that the contract states the conditions of discovery and the responsible party.

Other Considerations

Be sure to include in your contract architectural language that address percentage of work completed, in relationship to the scope of work to be completed. Even the best contractors have ways of getting dollars upfront in the building project, some are obvious and others are not. *Case in point, the contractor provides notarized "schedule of values" for drywall in the amount of $20,000.00. He has a total of 4200 square feet on the second floor and 1000 square feet on the first floor. He completes one half of the work on the first floor and submits a bill for 46.6% of work in place. The architect approves it and the draw request is forwarded to owner for signature.* The architect has not done his job and the contractor has taken advantage of the owner. But who should bear this cost, if the contractor walks or is fired? Also, be cautious by using architects from other states. The plans for certain things can be approved and rejected by the field inspector because the building standards used to construct the project are not consistent with SBC, IBC or a state modified building code.

If the key word for real estate is: location, location – then the key word for the building process is: discovery- discovery: from the concept through completion.

On each draw request, the architect should give the owner an inventory of all materials on the premises and a report on completed work as it is related to the total work scope. The data can be provided by the contractor and verified by the architect. In other words, the architect needs to be able to provide the owner with a snapshot of the progression of the project each time a "certificate for payment" is requested by the contractor. Also, if the contractor is dismissed, the architect may not be willing to do inventory of work scope. If the architect approves a "certificate for payment" and the work was not in place and the actual materials were not on premises, he will not change it at a later date. Therefore, make sure to include language in your contract that holds the architect liable for errors and omission for approved "certificates for payment".

Finally, make sure that you have in your contract the owner's right to make cosmetic changes without the architect's approval: floor covering, church signs, steeples, restroom fixtures, custom paint, molding and brand names of items. Often, people aren't fully cognitive of the possibilities until in a certain stage of the building project. The owner needs some flexibility to make changes without extra charges. Also, you need some type of language in your contract with the architect that allows the owner to waive non-structure and safety features on the final punch list. If this is not addressed, the architect can theoretically hold up the completion of the job by not authorizing the final payment and/or refusing to sign the "Certificate of Completion".

The Architectural Design Phase

The architectural design phase starts once the owner has agreed to fees to be charged and the owner and architect sign a contract. There are usually several steps in this process:

>Schematic Design Phase
>
>Design Development Phase
>
>Construction Documents Phase
>
>Bidding or Negotiation Phase
>
>Administration of the Construction Contract

Understanding your responsibilities and need to participate is crucial at this point. Too often, architects design projects without meaningful participation of the owner. When this happens, the owner has to live with a design that would have been approached differently.

Case in point, sometimes the owner is not made aware of critical terminologies. Sometimes, the owner is not allowed to discuss which name brand equipment is to be used. Does Trane or Carrier make the best HVAC system? What type or what brand of hardware should be used? As the owner, you need options; a good architect will share his knowledge and allow you to make sufficient input. What should be the weight of the carpet and can you change the weight? All of these concerns are addressed in the architect's written specifications of the plans. Once the specifications are issued and given to the contractor, it cannot be changed without the architect and it may require a codes official to sign-off. Therefore, I recommend that a person who understands the church needs and how the facility is to flow work with the architect in the initial stage of the plans.

Schematic Design Phase

The schematic phase allows the architect the opportunity to gain from the owner what is desired. Do you want offices with restrooms? Do you want a commercial kitchen? Do you want classrooms? In other words, you tell the architect what you want and he takes the information and fits it into the available square footage. Once he believes he has all of your information, he does a preliminary drawing.

The preliminary drawings have the bare minimum, meaning a three-dimensional view of the external structure, including grade and the size of rooms to be built. Be sure to scrutinize the drawings. The architect may have made the choir's rehearsal room too large and the choir's loft too small to accommodate your actual needs. Offices may be taking away from the classrooms' size. Make sure you understand the dimensions of all rooms before approving the preliminary drawings.

Design Development Phase

The design development phase involves licensed persons contributing to the developing of the plans. This phase is under the sole supervision of the architect. The plans take on life during this procedure. The architect, electrical engineer, civil engineer, mechanical engineer, and the structural engineer start adding their input with symbols and drawings subject to codes' requirements until everything becomes one document to be presented to codes for approval. During this phase, draftsmen are coming to the site to take measurements and to investigate the actual conditions.

Construction Documents Phase

During this phase, the architect is in consultation with codes' officials. When approved, required licensed persons stamp the plans. Depending upon each contributor, this process can take as long as a month. After each category of the plans are reviewed and approved, the architect stamps them. The architect gives the owner several copies of plans. At this point, the documents are ready for review by codes' plans and review departments. In some instances, the architect will provide the owner with plans stamped by the Fire Marshal's offices. These are called "permit-ready plans". However, in most instances, the plans are given to the general contractor to pull the permit and the contractor is responsible for getting plans reviewed and stamped. Personally, I recommend, "permit- ready plans". A copy of the Fire Marshal's plans is to remain on the premises until the owner receives a Use and Occupancy permit. Word of caution: do not allow the contractor or subcontractors to take the Fire Marshal's plans from the premises. I strongly suggest that the owner keep these plans secure at all times. If you dismiss the contractor, he will most likely take your approved-stamped plans. If the original contractor is dismissed and the stamped plans cannot be located for the new contractor, a new set of plans must be reviewed. In some instances, new requirements may be requested by codes before approving the same plans.

Bidding or Negotiation Phase

The architect will assist you with the bid process. He or she is responsible for making sure that each bidding contractor is comparing "apples with apples." The gauge of steel, the grade of lumber, the warranty on shingles can cause a bid to be high or low. Also, the architect with the owner pre-determines when all bids are to be received and opened. Usually, the architect will take care of this process completely unless there is a conflict of interest.

If the project is not bidden, it should be negotiated. The project's negotiation terms are determined by the type of contract to be used by the general contractor. Sometimes, the architect will assist the owner with this endeavor for additional fees. I strongly suggest using the architect as a negotiator if you do not have a lawyer.

Administration of the Construction Contract

In addition to a notarized bid, the general contractor is required to submit to the lending institution, owner, and architect a notarized schedule of values. This is a breakdown of the bid amount according to categories such as demolition, roofing, plumbing, general conditions, framing and etc.

It is the responsibility of the architect to make sure that the general contractor only receives payments for work in place in proportion to the total line items. For example, the contractor bids $44,000.00 for general conditions. The first month, he requests $15,000.00. The total contract is $370,000. Therefore, he is charging approximately $7.40 per thousands for general conditions ($326,000.00/$44,000.00). If at the time of the request only 5% of the total contract is completed, the payment request represents 29% of work not in place. Make sure that you scrutinize draw requests (certificate for payment); the administration of the construction contract deals with payments to the contractor and making sure that contractor is building according to plans.

Please, do not allow the architect to pay the contractor funds for work not in place. If you do, you may not recover your funds and the architect will argue that you agreed because you signed the request for payments.

Sometimes, the architect will offer additional services for a fee over the design cost. Some of the services are:

>Construction Budget Analysis
>
>Plan Revisions
>
>Project Manager
>
>Reproduction of plans

The Construction Budget Analysis

It is my experience that the Construction Budget Analysis can be useless. Most times, a builder will use a square foot cost. This is an estimate and not the best estimate. In my opinion, it has no value other than to give to the bank a proposed cost of the project. You can save yourself some out-of pocket expense by using my formula in Chapter Three or an online square foot cost analysis.

If cost is the primary factor, you will need priced plans. The difference is: a bid is an official process that involves the owner and architect in a process that requires a set date and an award date.

Plan Revisions

If not addressed, plan revisions can be costly. Most architects reserve the right to charge additional fees to make changes to the plans once they are approved. The owner needs to make sure that any revision caused by the architect's error, codes' field inspectors, Fire Marshal's inspectors or the general contract's concessions, is not the owner's responsibility.

The Project Manager

A project manager is a person who is responsible to protect the interest of another such as: an owner, architect or general contractor. Projects less than a million dollars may not require an architect's project manager. Every project should have a general contractor's project manager that supervises subcontractors, and all integrity of plans, labor, and materials. The owner should have a project manager that makes sure that the contractor's project manager is doing his job.

Reproduction of Plans

The plans are usually the architect's property, meaning that copyrights belong to the architect. In some instances, plans are the property of the owners. If the plans are the property of the architect, you will be charged for additional copies. This can be expensive depending upon the cost and number of additional copies needed.

It is recommended that the architect's fees include a minimum number of copies based upon the categories of work to be performed: excavation, foundation, framing, roofing, electrical, plumbing, low voltage wiring, drywall, etc.

Chapter Four

Questions for Discussion

1. For building purpose, who officially starts it?

2. What are some of the things that a good architect will do for your project?

3. Are all architects alike?

4. List some reasons that make an architect unusual.

5. Name several ways an architect can be located.

6. What is the purpose of an investigative form letter?

7. During the building process the architect is to protect whom?

8. Does an architect need insurance?

9. Who is responsible for the mechanical engineer's drawings in a

plan?

10. What are discoveries?

11. What is a construction budget analysis?

12. Does it make a difference if the architect is from a different state?

13. What is the responsibility of a project manager?

Chapter 5

The Middle Passage
"A Moment of Reflectivity"

Most building projects are fueled by excitement, anticipation, and determination. However, before you sign a contract to build, you need to calm down. Why? Well, you need a moment to reflect. Like an airplane, you might be on the runway, but you are not committed to take off until you start down the runway. The same is true with building: having secured funds in hand and approved plans put you on the runway, but you are not committed to build until you sign a contract with a construction company. When you sign a contract to build, potential headaches, disappointments, and lawsuits are waiting to whistle.

I recommend that the committee in place meet and discuss:

A Contingency Plan

Extra Funding Potentials

Cost of Furniture

Cost of Additional Safety Equipment

Cost of Additional Landscape Needs

Aesthetics Cost

Re-think How the Facility Will Be Used

Commitment to Build

Insurance

Explanations:

Contingency Plan

A contingency plan is a "what if plan". It is highly unlikely that your project will be finished without some unexpected problems. Taking time to role-play some negatives will aid your contingency plan.

Additional Funds

Being prepared to secure additional funds is a necessity. Most architects and general contractors will tell you upfront that you need from 5 to 20 percent contingency fund capacity. I know of very few buildings that were built under-budget. If your project is projected to cost $700,000.00, you need at least $70,000.00 contingency capacity.

Furnishings

When I sold auto insurance, it was common to see people who had the down payment for the car and did not have a down payment for the insurance. Also, it is common to see churches whose lovely and spacious conference rooms and classrooms have no furniture or inadequate furniture. I recommend that once you start building that you start the process of acquiring the necessary furnishings. Stores may be willing to negotiate storage without cost.

Safety Equipment

We live in a world that demands safety. Even in the church, ungodly men and women are waiting to take advantage of every perceived weakness. Child molestation is not off limits to religious organizations. The church member is not excluded from the usage or sale of dope. A church that has more than one hallway might need to consider security cameras. Parking lots, as well, need to be secured for the safety of people.

Landscape

Landscaping is not part of the plans unless codes demand it. However, this does not excuse the fact that churches need to plan for landscaping. The proper landscape adds beauty and some value to a building. Without it, it is like a man putting on new suits with run-down shoes.

Aesthetics Cost

Walls can be clothed with beautiful art work. Nothing brings warmth to the interior of a building like pictures and plants. Be sure to consider aesthetic costs.

Re-visiting the Vision

Re-thinking the use of the facility will allow you to add small things without changing the plans for little or no cost. Brackets for televisions, additional wall plugs, and data conduits are sometimes over-looked initially.

Commitment to Build

Nothing is worst than having people standing around talking about why we should have waited. I strongly suggest that you have committed people before you hire the contractor. Make sure that the membership is ready. Make sure that you have the financial support of your supportive members.

Insurance

Having the right insurance in place can save you some sleepless nights. As the owner, you will need to provide a builder-risk policy if the contractor does not carry a floater. A builder-risk or floater protects materials and uncompleted structures during the building process. Also, you may need contractual insurance. I strongly advise owners to call their insurance agent to make sure that the right coverage is in place.

If you are satisfied with your reflective analysis, you are ready to build. Next, you need to consider the type of contract to be used and find a general contractor.

Types of Contracts

There are several types of contracts that can be used between the owner and a general contractor. It is wise to insist that the general contractor uses some type of AIA contract. Some architects will provide a preferred contract to be used. Types of contracts will be discussed in a later chapter.

Chapter Five

Questions for Discussion

1. Have we done our due diligence?

2. Do we have the resolve to build in conflict?

3. Are the members prepared?

4. Do we have additional needs for the facility?

5. What are our contingency plans?

6. Are we prepared to buy the furnishings?

7. Do we have in place a décor committee?

8. Which type of contract should we use?

Chapter 6

The General Contractor

There are approximately 1800 licensed general contractors in the State of Tennessee. According to the California State Licensing Board, the construction industry is the single largest market in the United States. It is believed that approximately 20,000 contractors are licensed each year.

In Tennessee and most states, a contractor is only required to be licensed if the project's cost exceeds a stated dollar amount or the project involves a health hazard to the general population. *In other words, it might cost $12,000.00 to build a walkway across Indian Creek but only a licensed contractor would be considered by the state.* Also, subcontractors are required to be licensed for some trades such as electrical and plumbing. If you do not know the requirements for licensing and the stated amount that requires a contractor to be licensed in your state, call the state's licensing board. You can find the states' web page addresses in appendix 3.

A general contractor may be licensed as an individual, partnership, or corporation. The business may be in an individual name or a generic name. However, most businesses are in a generic name and are usually incorporated. Sometimes, the owner will use his or her name to incorporate.

Because of the nature of a corporation, the true owner is not known. The president of a corporation is not necessarily the person calling the play. A corporation has board members. The board members are responsible for the decisions of the corporation. However, in a corporation for profit, the person that has the most stock in the company can persuade the decision of the board and not choose to be the president.

Businesses choose to incorporate to protect individual stockholders, and board members from potential liabilities of doing business. In most instances, it is hard to remove the protected shield of a corporation: meaning that the corporation's assets are the only properties subject to lawsuits or judgments, thus giving corporations, in some instances, a license to victimize the community without serious consequences.

Therefore, it is very important to do "due diligence" when doing business with a corporation. The following information should be required of a corporation:

> The current status of the corporation verified by the Secretary of State
>
> The principal officers of operation
>
> A certified and notarized resolution of the board's minutes to engage in a contractual relationship
>
> The address where the meeting took place and the name of board members present
>
> A certified and notarized excerpt of minutes that the person signing for the company has binding authority to represent the company as an individual in the capacity of signature
>
> A current certified financial statement and an income and expense statement
>
> The name of the business' legal counsel

Explanations

Corporation's Status

Every state requires a corporation to file an annual report. The filing seeks to verify changes and ask for the officers and board members names and addresses. In most states, if the information is not returned, the corporation status will be revoked. Depending upon which state you are in, this can be a major or minor violation. If the corporation is sued, having the name of officers and board member is a plus. Never do business with a corporation whose status has been revoked unless the company can have its status administratively reinstated. Otherwise, you may be getting ready to bite into a rotten apple. If a corporation is too apathetic to return a simple form and pay a very small filing fee, this is an indication of their inability to manage your building project.

The Principal Location

You need to know the principal location of operation. In other words, the business office, the warehouse, and equipment storage sheds. Just like there are many paper-mills schools that give beautiful diplomas from P.O. Boxes -- there are a myriad of "paper-mill general contractors." They advertise invisible services and make sweet and tempting promises of delusion.

Corporation's Resolution

Every corporation that operates according to standard business practices, have minutes. These corporations usually have minutes stating a disposition before an action is taken. The owner should always require a resolution from the board approving the company to enter into a contractual relationship. The secretary of the corporation should sign the resolution. Also, it should be notarized.

Place of Meeting

The place of the meeting is important. If you need to prove that minutes are the creative imagination of a person or persons, knowing where the meeting took place allows your legal council the opportunity to verify attendance. Sometimes presidents or secretaries make up minutes to fit the occasion and declare that invisible people showed up.

Statement of Authorization

It is regrettable, but we live at a time when you cannot be too cautious. Anytime a person signs for a company, a binding statement should always accompany that person's signature. In other words, the signing person should have the authority to bind the company as an individual. A corporation cannot sign a contract; a person must sign for it. Therefore, have your legal council to prepare the necessary form. This form should be included as an amendment to the contract to perform the work of the project.

Certified Financial Records

As the owner, you should require the corporation's current financial statement and revenue statements. The financial statement gives a snapshot of the corporation's types of assets and the amount of assets. The revenue statement allows you to determine the cash flow of a business by looking at the incomes and expenses, and it allows you to identify business practices. For example, the financial statement may show a large amount of equipment as asset but the revenue statement does not show insurance premiums. If a large percentage of the assets are accounts receivables, it allows you the opportunity to request additional information concerning the likelihood and nature of collectivity:

> *Are these contractual receipts?*
>
> *Are these disputed receipts?*
>
> *What are the names and addresses of the accounts and who are the contact persons?*

Name of Legal Council

Knowing the general contractor's legal council can be beneficial. Sometimes, a corporation may have financial backers who are not stockholders. Sometimes, a lawyer may be registrar of agent for a corporation. Having knowledge of the facts can keep you alert regarding potential conflicts of interests.

General Considerations

The above due diligence procedures should be used with any type or style of business when pursuing a contractual relationship.

Again, do not pay a contractor for work that is not in place. Do not make down payments for materials. Why? If you have signed a contract, the contractor has a security lien on your property until you satisfy the terms of the contract. If the contractor cannot afford to buy the materials and be paid upon delivery, you buy the materials. Why? Most contractors will charge you a mark-up and a delivery charge. In most instances, they will not choose the best quality of materials. Not having the ability to obtain credit for materials is a red flag that speaks to credit worthiness.

Also, a corporation that does not have at least 25% of the projected building cost in tangible assets should not be used unless the president of the company signs as an individual and the project is fully bonded for performance.

Chapter Six

Questions for Discussion

1. Is a license required for subcontractors?

2. Why do contractors incorporate their companies?

3. What should I be looking for on the contractor's financial statement?

4. What does the revenue statement tell about the contractor?

5. Is it a good business practice to pay a contractor a down payment before the work starts?

6. Is it a good business practice to pay the contractor for materials before they are delivered?

7. What additional information do you need to know about the contractor's accounts receivables?

Chapter 7

Finding the Right Contractor

It is commonly believed that contractors who have performed well for others can be trusted. This is far from the truth. **Contractors often have serious cash flow problems.** *For example, they may have two or more Peters to rob at a given time, however, when they get to your job; there is not a Peter to be found.* Two things will happen: they will go bankrupt or the quality of workmanship will suffer. Construction work can be seasonal and highly competitive. It is strongly recommended that an investigative approach be used to secure a contractor. Don't rush the construction process without taking time to do due diligence. If it takes two months to interview potential contractors, spend the time. It will prove to be beneficial.

Whereas large corporations are constantly building, churches and individuals are not usually well-versed when it comes to the building industry. Therefore, a bid does not guarantee that you will end up with the best general contractor for your project. Contractors do not apply the same logic to each job! They know the ropes. They know what they can get away with and they know when to roll the dices. *This is not to say that there are no honest contractors, but finding one will require some effort.*

Fact Sheet for Securing a Contractor

1. Building experience
2. General Contractor's experience
3. Reputation in the building industry
4. Credit Worthiness
5. Status of license from the date of issuance

Explanation:

Building Experience

There is a myriad of "paper-mill general contractors". They have little or no knowledge of the actual building trade and no skills' experience. They have the intelligentsia; they have the required access to secure a license due to the right connections. If the general contractor does not know the building trade, the contractor is limited. The contractor cannot assist the architect or the subcontractor in the day-to-day construction of the project. You need a general contractor with some years of actual building skills.

General Contractor's Experience

Not only does the contractor need personal experience and skills of the building trade but also he or she needs some years in the business as a general contractor. Often, the project will face some codes' challenges; having an experienced general contactor is beneficial in crises. Sometimes field inspectors do not allow what is on the paper in the actual building of a project. An experienced contractor will be able to suggest an alternate idea in the field.

Building Industry's Reputation

You need a general contractor that has a good reputation. The quality of work is directly tied to the integrity of the general contractor. If the contractor is a person or company that does not pay its subcontractors timely, most likely your project will have subcontractors with little or no integrity for workmanship quality. In other words, you will end-up with people looking to take every short cut, covering up, and having no respect for others on the job. Case in point, the drywall person might not protect the painter's work. The electrician might cut and not repair holes in the drywall. Therefore, you need a contractor that has a good reputation.

Credit Worthiness

You need a contractor who has good credit. A contractor that has good credit intends to do right. A contractor who has good credit has good managerial skills. A good contractor is one that knows how to manage people and money.

Status of License

You need to check the license status of the general contractor. You need to check for complaints and any type of negative actions of the state's licensing board, such as suspensions or delays to renew.

How to Find the Right Contractor

Illustration 12

Yellow Page

Owners

Building Vendors

Architects

Subcontractors

Commercial Loan Officers of Banks

Examples of Inquiry Letters

Illustration 13

Letter to Potential Contractor

Dear:

Our organization has voted to build a new sanctuary with classrooms and a family life center. We have a letter of intent from a local bank to acquire funds to build. We have decided to bid the project among three or five selected contractors. The estimated cost of the project is $1,050,000.00.

Your firm was recommended to us by _____ (or, your firm is being considered because of your advertisement in the yellow pages). If you have an interest in bidding on this project, would you be so kind as to forward to us the requested information:

How many years in business as a general contractor?
_____

How many years of building experience?
_____

Are you a member of the Better Business Bureau or a trade association?
_____

Is your license current?
_____

What is your license capacity?
_____

Can your company provide a performance bond?
_____

Does your firm carry comprehensive general liability and workman compensation insurance?

Can your company provide the lending institution certified financial records by a CPA, if awarded the bid? Yes or No

Please provide the names, addresses and phone numbers of three subcontractors that you have worked with in the last two years.

Please provide the names, addresses and phone numbers for the contact person of three projects that your firm built within the last two years.

Please provide the names, addresses and phone numbers of three building supply vendors with whom your company has an account.

Please provide the name and address of your primary bank.

Contractor's Signature

Cordially,

Illustration 14

Letter to Subcontractors

Dear

    Douglas & Sons Construction Company listed you as one of the subcontractors that they have contracted within the last two years. Would you be so kind as to complete our questionnaire? All information shared with us will be kept confidential. Please return in the postage-paid envelope.

1. Does the above general contractor use your company regularly?

   _____

2. Does the above general contractor use a written contract for subcontractors?

   _____

3. Does the general contractor require subcontractors to sign a conditional lien release on each draw request?

   _____

4. Does the general contractor use a written payment schedule to pay subcontractors?

   _____

5. Has the general contractor ever asked you to wait for a payment for work completed?

   _____

6. Has the above general contractor ever asked you to contract with the owner for a job within his scope of work?

   _____

7. Does the general contractor purchase materials for the subcontractors?

   _____

8. Has the owner or the owner's lending institution ever paid you for a job within the general contractor's scope of work?

   _____

9. When changes were required on the job, did the general contractor or the contractor's project manager have sufficient knowledge of facts to execute a proper alternative?

   _____

Illustration 15

Owner's Reference

Dear

Douglas & Sons Construction Company listed you as a recent client. We are considering this firm for a building project. Would you be so kind as to take a moment and complete the questionnaire? Your reply will be treated with confidentiality. Please return it in the postage-paid envelope.

1. Was this a bid project?

2. Was this the lowest bid?

3. Was the project managed well by the contractor?

4. Did the contractor use skilled subcontractors?

5. Did you have any "change orders" disputes?

6. Where subcontractors paid timely?

7. Was the job completed on time or before schedule?

8. Did the contractor provide a performance bond?

9. Did the contractor maintain insurance on the project without lapse of coverage?

10. Were you totally pleased with the finished product?

11. Were suppliers paid timely?

_____

12. Did the contractor use temporary laborers?

_____

13. Did the contractor provide laborers with proper tools and safety equipment?

_____

14. Did the contractor provide you with the names of the subcontractors?

_____

Illustration 16

Letter to Suppliers

Dear

    Douglas & Sons Construction Company listed you, as a vendor for their company. Would you be so kind as to complete our questionnaire? All information shared with us will be kept confidential. Please return in the postage-paid envelope.

1. Does the above company have an open-ended account with your company?

_____

2. Does the above company have a charge account with a limit above $50,000.00?

_____

3. Does the above company have a charge account with a limit above $25,000.00?

_____

4. Approximately how many years has the account been open?

_____

5. Are accounts maintained properly?

_____

Evaluating the Contractor

Interpreting responses to your inquiry is subjective; however, the suggested key is based upon personal experience and information shared by vendors, other general contractors, subcontractors, banks, architects, and owners. Please feel free to interpret your findings based upon location and other means. For the sake of space and time, I will use: positive, caution and negative to grade a response. Positive = precede; Caution = more information needed; Negative = do not consider. If a potential contractor receives three or more negatives, the contractor is not a good candidate.

Evaluation Key

Contractor's Inquiry

Question #	Answer	Grade
How many years in business as a general contractor?		
1	Less than 10 #yrs	Caution
1	Less than 3 #yrs	Negative
1	More than 10 #yrs	Positive
How many years of building experience?		
2	Less than 10 #yrs	Caution
2	Less than 7 #yrs	Negative
2	More than 10 #yrs	Positive

Question #	Answer	Grade

Are you a member of the Better Business Bureau or a trade group?

3	No	Caution
3	Yes	Positive

Is your license current?

4	No	Negative
4	Yes	Positive

What is your license capacity?

5	50-450 thousand	Caution
5	450 thousand and over	Positive

Can your company provide a performance bond?

6	No	Negative
6	Yes	Positive

Does your firm carry comprehensive general liability and workman compensation insurance?

7	No	Negative
7	Yes	Positive

Can your company provide the lending institution certified records by a CPA, if awarded the bid?

8	No	Negative
8	Yes	Positive

| Question # | Answer | Grade |

Evaluation Key

Subcontractors' Inquiry

Does the above general contractor use your company regularly?

1	No	Caution
1	Yes	Positive

Does the above general contractor use a written contract for subcontractors?

2	No	Negative
2	Yes	Positive

Does the above general contractor require subcontractors to sign a conditional lien release on each draw request?

3	No	Negative
3	Yes	Positive

Does the general contractor use a written payment schedule to pay subcontractors?

4	No	Caution
4	Yes	Positive

Has the general contractor ever asked you to wait for a payment for work completed?

5	Yes	Caution
5	No	Positive

| Question # | Answer | Grade |

Has the above general contractor ever asked you to contract with the owner for a job within his scope of work?

6	No	Positive
6	Yes	Caution

Does the general contractor purchase materials for the subcontractors?

7	No	Caution
7	Yes	Positive

Has the owner or the owner's lending institution ever paid you for a job within the general contractor's scope of work?

8	No	Positive
8	Yes	Negative

When changes were required on the jobs, did the general contractor or the contractor's project manager have sufficient knowledge of facts to execute a proper alternative?

9	No	Negative
9	Yes	Positive

Evaluation Key
Owners' Inquiry

Was this a bid project?

1	No	Caution
1	Yes	Positive

Question #	Answer	Grade
Was this the lowest bid?		
2	No	Positive
2	Yes	Caution
Was the project managed well by the contractor?		
3	No	Negative
3	Yes	Positive
Did the contractor use skilled subcontractors?		
4	No	Negative
4	Yes	Positive
Did you have any "change orders" disputes?		
5	No	Positive
5	Yes	Caution
Were subcontractors paid timely?		
6	No	Negative
6	Yes	Positive
Did the contractor provide you the names of the subcontractors working on your project?		
7	No	Caution
7	Yes	Positive

Question #	Answer	Grade

Was the job completed on schedule or before schedule?

8	No	Caution
8	Yes	Positive

Did the contractor provide a performance bond for this project?

9	No	Caution
9	Yes	Positive

Did the contractor maintain insurance on the project without lapse of coverage?

10	No	Negative
10	Yes	Positive

Were you totally pleased with the finished product?

11	No	Caution
11	Yes	Positive

Were suppliers paid timely?

12	No	Negative
12	Yes	Positive

Did the contractor use temporary laborers?

13	No	Positive
13	Yes	Caution

| Question # | Answer | Grade |

Did the contractor provide laborers with proper tools and safety equipment?

14	No	Negative
14	Yes	Positive

Evaluation Key

Suppliers' Inquiry

Does the above company have an open-ended account with your company?

1	No	Caution
1	Yes	Positive

Does the above company have a charge account with a limit above $50,000.00?

2	No	Caution
2	Yes	Positive

Does the above company have a charge account with a limit above $25,000.00?

3	No	Negative
3	Yes	Caution

How many years has the account been open?

4	New	Caution
4	2-5 Yrs	Caution
4	5 + Yrs	Positive

Question #	Answer	Grade
Are accounts maintained properly?		
5	No	Negative
5	Yes	Positive

Evaluation's Results

The number of "Cautions" _____

The number of "Negatives" _____

The number of "Positives" _____

The Bid Process

The architect with the owner's approval should establish the bid procedure. The contractor will need plans to bid the job. The owner is responsible for providing plans to each contractor that bids on the project. If you do not have a budget for extra plans, the cost has to be absorbed by the awarded contractor. If this is not agreeable, provide each contractor with one set of plans. The contractor will need at least 45 days to present a quality bid. However, you do not need to bid the job.

If you are satisfied with your due diligence, you can negotiate a contract amount. You would need the advice of a lawyer and/or the architect to advance this process. However, for most owners, it would be best to bid the project among selected general contractors.

Awarding of the Contract

If you have adhered to the suggested procedures for finding the right contractor, you are ready for the signing of the contract. The contractor will present you a contract to sign. Before signing the contract, several important items need to be addressed:

1. A copy of the contractor's current license

2. A copy of the contractor's applicable insurance policies naming the owner as an additional insured and a letter of intent from the contractor's insurance company that a performance bond will be issued upon the signing of the contract. Also, be sure that the contractor's liability policy is comprehensive and does not limit the scope of liability to a specific class of work. In addition, make sure that the contractor's insurance protects you from damages caused by the contractors or subcontractors defective work such as: water damages, fire, collapse and etc.

3. Certified financial records by a CPA

4. The reviewing of the contract by your legal counsel

5. Making sure that language in the contracts gives the owner flexibility and authority to act and protect its interest. See Chapter Eight, Subtopic: **A Good Contract Should Include:**

6. Notarized schedule of values detailing cost and categories of work to be performed that equal the total bid amount. Some contractors will include schedule of values with the bid.

7. A tentative list of subcontractors to be used on your project.

8. How and who will purchase materials? I recommend that a system be used that allows the church or other tax exempted entities to receive tax savings.

9. A meeting with architect, owner, consultants, project managers, and bank officials to review plans, to determine pay schedule and to determine who will represent the owner for the day-to-day decisions and instructions

10. If you are borrowing funds to build your project, do not sign a contract until the contractor provides a schedule of values to the lending institution.

Chapter Seven

Questions for Discussion

1. Why shouldn't previous work be used as the sole standard for evaluating a general contractor?

2. Why shouldn't the construction process be rushed?

3. Name several things that should be considered in seeking a potential contractor.

4. What is a paper-mill contractor?

5. Why does a general contractor need a good reputation?

6. Name several ways to find the right contractor.

7. If a contractor receives three or more negative scores, what should you do?

8. What is the minimum amount of days a contractor needs to bid a job?

9. Name several things that need to be addressed before signing the general contractor's contract.

Chapter 8

Construction Contracts

Using the right contract for your project is just as important as finding the right general contractor to build your project. Be aware of homemade contracts. Whenever you enter into a contractual relationship, you need a written contract. Even if parties are related, if the contractual performance will impact, directly or indirectly, two or more persons, you need a written contract.

The contract empowers the contractor to perform his work according to documents relating to building initiatives on the owner's behalf. It states the contractor's rights for payments. It defines the scope of work to be completed. Also, it protects the owners. It allows the owner to expect a standard of performance according to the architect's plans and building ethics. It gives the owner the right to terminate the contractual relationship if the contractor should do anything that is unethical or violates the terms of the contract. Therefore, because of the complexity of contracts, a lawyer should read and make modifications to a contract before it is signed.

A word of wisdom, do not be afraid to negotiate the language and terminology of a contract. Hopefully, the project will be completed without any serious bumps. A good contract is like having insurance; you do not need it until a specific crisis and than it's too late to buy. The same is true of a contract: you don't need a contract until you have problems. Therefore, get it right upfront!

A construction contract is a legal document which specifies the what-when-where-how-how much- what if-no and the why not. A good contract should include the following.

A Good Contract Should Include:

1. A copy of the contractor's license or the registration number
2. A statement of work ethics and quality of workmanship
3. An addendum declaring the plans as a part of the contract.
4. A timetable for starting and completing the project.
5. A penalty clause for not completing the job on schedule
6. A bonus for completing the job ahead of schedule
7. A fixed price for the work including labor, fees and materials
8. A payment schedule
9. A clause that deals with 'change orders" and damage to existing structure, if applicable.
10. A clause that outlines how disputes will be resolved
11. A clause that allows the owner to terminate the contract and pay for only architecturally approved work in place without mediation.
12. Warrantee statements for workmanship and purchased materials
13. A clause that demands names of all subcontractors and vendors for the project be given to owner and if not, it can be grounds for terminating the contract.
14. The owner's rights to sublet work to certain qualifying groups or persons
15. A clause that demands conditional mechanic's liens releases before payment.

16. Insurance requirements and penalties for lapse of coverage

17. Owner's rights to terminate contract without mediation of architect, or lending institution consent for specified reasons

18. Specific reasons for termination of contract: unwillingness to make immediate repairs for damage to existing structure, lapse of insurance policies or policy, any type of fraud, not paying subcontractors or any person that has mechanic's liens rights, not paying or writing vendors worthless checks for materials used in the construction of facility, and the creation of health hazards, to name a few.

Type of Contracts

Most lending institutions will require some type of American Institute of Architects' contract to be used. There are several categories:

>Cost Plus
>
>Construction Management
>
>Design-Build
>
>Owner and Contractor
>
>Owner and Project Manager

Design-Build Approach

Some architects are builders or may have ownership in a construction company. In these instances, the architect will offer his services under a contract that deals with "design and build". There are several reasons for this approach: the architect will reduce fees for the design if he is allowed to build the project; the flow of the design is less text-bookish when a builder and architect work together on the drawings. However, if the cost to build is not bidden, you will not know the true saving. Also, the "design-build" concept has the greatest possibility for conflicts of interests. In addition to having a lawyer to view the contract, the following steps are recommended: have a no-mediation clause to dismiss the general contactor; a clause that states the lack of discovery is the sole responsibility of general contractor and architect; and a clause that states that the architect is to provide services for the project at no additional cost, if the contractor is dismissed.

Because contracts are legal documents, it is best that you ask your architect for a suggested contract and take it to your lawyer for approval. Personally, I prefer the standard owner and contractor's contract. For more information about American Institute of Architects' contracts, you may visit their web site: http://www.aia.org/nav_atp or if you wish to purchase their forms, you may visit: http://www.constructionbook.com. The contracts may be purchased online.

Chapter Eight

Questions for Discussion

1. What authority does the contract give the contractor?

   _____
   _____

2. What expectations does the contract give the owner?

   _____
   _____

3. Why should a lawyer be used before signing a contract?

   _____
   _____

4. The contract is what type of document?

5. Name some items that should be included in a good contract.

6. What is a design-build contract?

7. What are the advantages of a design-build contract?

8. What are the disadvantages of a design-build contract?

Chapter 9

The Building Project and Church Members

The largest capital expenditure of most churches is the church's building initiatives. Yet, most churches fail to use this initiative to strengthen loyalty among its membership. For the most part, not one cent of the building expenditures will directly go into the pocket of a church member.

It is my belief that the church should never enter a building project without considering how it can strengthen the **wealth** of its members. Cases in point, if your church has one of the best carpet installers, why not make sure that he or she is awarded the job. If you have a professional painter in the church, why not make sure that the painting is awarded to qualified members. In other words, make sure that subcontracted work is awarded to qualified members of your church, especially if they are supportive of the financial thrust of the church.

The Bible set forth two principles that should impact the church's leadership: *"we have not because we ask not; "God's people perish because of the lack of knowledge."* While there seem to be an awareness that a percentage of local, state, and federal agencies' projects should be awarded to defined groups, too many minority churches build without demanding minority participation. However, the denial of membership participation is not limited to minority churches. A disconnect exists among most churches as it relates to membership participation in its building projects.

Why? Some say it is not about black or white. Others cite possible conflict of interests. Some people believe that envy and jealousy, "the crab mentality," hinder membership participation.

Regardless of the reason, it is foolish to take food off your plate to feed others while your family dies of malnutrition. The church is a champion of social justice. Therefore, it is hypocrisy to demand of others what you refuse to do for yourself. The Bible teaches that those who fail to provide for their families are worse than infidels.

It is my opinion that when members are given an opportunity to participate in the building project, it builds and strengthens loyalty among the membership. However, it needs to be well-structured.

Making It Happen:

1. Make sure that your contract has language that demands a percentage of minority subcontractors or the owner's right to choose subcontractors.

2. Do a survey of entrepreneurs within the congregation.

3. Allow the entrepreneurs to bid labor and material cost with the general contractor or negotiate the cost with the church.

4. Have the entrepreneurs to understand that he or she will be held to standard building codes and ethics.

5. Prepare to purchase workman compensation insurance.

6. Be prepared to reject members that do not have the capacity to do the job in a timely and professional manner.

7. Don't expect members to make unreasonable concessions.

It is sad that most of us allow negativity to persuade us rather than hope. It is easy to name ten or more reasons why members should not be used in the building project. However, I am convinced that one positive can outweigh all the negatives.

The church's tithes come from members. Therefore, when faithful and qualified members have the opportunity to participate in the building project, it is God's way of opening up windows of blessings. God says to us," try me!" Unfortunately, most of us only have one idea in mind. That is, "give God some money and he will give you more money." I suggest that God demands a giving of opportunities as well as money. When we give God our mind, body and soul, he is committed to giving us things. The Bible teaches that He knows our needs.

The church is called to model Godly behavior. It is a sad contradiction of whose we are and whom we represent when we teach one thing and do another. Every pulpit echoes the theme of giving, yet, when presented the opportunity to give back to the very people we preach to - too often we fail.

In many instances, the church is guilty of working its oxen with muzzles. When we ask members to give to building projects and refuse to allow participation solely because they are members, we have worked the member oxen without needed provisions. It is time that the church educates itself. The church is called to lead in every Godly human pursuit.

If given the opportunity, engage your qualified members in the fruits of your building initiatives.

Chapter Nine

Questions for Discussion

1. Involving qualified members in the building initiative stimulates which attributes among members?

2. The building initiative should be viewed as an opportunity to strengthen which needs of members?

3. What do most churches fail to do as it relates to social awareness and involvement?

4. Name several things that need to be considered to involve members in the building initiative.

5. What is a practical way of implementing Malachi 3:10?

6. As it relates to building initiatives, why are some churches guilty of violating scripture?

7. The church is called to model what can of behavior?

Chapter 10

Building Your Vision

When the contractor posts a building permit on your premises, the ideas, hopes, and aspirations of the vision begin to take on character and structure. For some, this will be a labor of joy but for others it will be a momentary nightmare.

It is at this point that many of the "nay-Sayers" say, "I didn't believe it but I see it." People are feeling good about their input in the project. The contractor has a smile on his or her face. Neighbors and other church families are happy and take time to extend pre-dedicatory expressions. *In other words, everybody is drinking your Kool-Aid.*

Believe me! This is not the time to celebrate. This is not the time to shout and declare victory. Unlike the poet, it is best that you wait for the battle to be over before shouting. In thirty days, the contractor will need to be paid. In some instances, subcontractors have paid their labor force and need their money like wild dogs need flea collars. If the general contractor has to wait to receive a draw to pay subcontractors, you can bet that he or she knows how to manipulate and massage the "schedule of values" to his or her advantage. In most instances, the contractor has built-in manipulations. In the building trade, this is called **"top heavy contracts"**.

The Bible teaches that Christians are to be sober and vigilant. This is the time to sleep with one eye open and one eye closed. This is the time to be on guard for the devil who is seeking whom he may devour. This is the time to hold everybody accountable and responsible to the integrity of the project.

Accountability

Accountability is defined as answerable to another. It is the action of one being scrutinized by another. It is subordinate in character, while being proactive in duty. In other words, to be accountable is to be responsible.

Illustration 17

An Accountability Chart

Banks	(are accountable to)	Stockholders
		Regulatory Agencies
Owners	(are accountable to)	Lenders
		Members and Codes
Architects	(are accountable to)	Licensing Agencies
		Owners
		Codes
Contractors	(are accountable to)	Owners
		Architects
		Licensing Agencies
		Codes

In this chart, the organization is accountable to lenders, membership and codes. The bank is accountable to its stockholders and regulatory agencies. The architect is accountable to licensing agencies, owner and codes. The contractor is accountable to the owner, architect, licensing agencies and codes.

If you borrow funds from a lending institution, get ready to pay a sum of fees at the closing. The bank will require an appraisal. Remodeling or attaching to an existing structure requires hazard inspections. It is easy for a bank to charge from $2,000.00 to $20,000.00 in fees that are required by banking regulations. Some banks will insist that owners hire a consultant to protect their interest at the owner's cost.

Even though the owner contracts with the architect, the architect is accountable to the state and local agencies that issued and recognized his or her license. *For instance, an architect may say to a client, "you do not want me to do a punch list."* The reason could be there are cosmetic and/or non-safety issues that were not addressed according to plans. If the architect gives the information to the owner or contractor, it has to be acted upon.

While building our church, the first general contractor, whom we had to dismiss, was trying to get more funds for demolition. So, he casually suggested that the insulation might be asbestos. *The architect stopped the meeting and said to the contractor, "Stop the project and have the material tested!" even though, we had earlier paid for the testing of floors and ceiling tiles materials.* The architect's license was at risk when the contractor made known his wild suspicion of asbestos.

Second, the architect is accountable to the owner. The architect is accountable to the owner by making sure that:

> The plans meet all codes, local, state, and federal
>
> The building is built according to plans.
>
> No funds are paid for work not in place.
>
> On-site inspection of construction
>
> Owner has a list of subcontractors.

The contractor is primarily responsible to the architect. He is to build the project according to the plans and specifications without deviating. Any deviations should be at the owner's request with the architect's approval. With non-structural and non-safety issues, the architect will usually grant the owner's request without changing the plans. However, the contractor will be responsible to give the owner, at the end the project, a copy of "as-is drawings". Also, the contractor might request a change to keep the project in budget or other problems due to construction's discoveries. Under no circumstance can the contractor deviate from the plans without the architect's approval.

Sometimes, contractors will under bid a project and cry on the architect's shoulders. Be sure that the architect knows that you choose to be informed of all changes requested by the contractor. Some contractors use "change orders" to get additional funds out of a job. It is best that you have in your contract a clause that addresses "change orders". I suggest language that states, "Change orders" are not valid until the owner, the architect and the contractor have signed it"

Chapter Ten

Questions for Discussion

1. When does the vision take on character and structure?

   _____

   _____

2. Why isn't it wise to allow jubilation to override cautiousness at the posting of a building permit?

   _____

   _____

3. What is the definition of accountability?

   _____

   _____

4. The bank is accountable to whom?

   _____

   _____

5. The architect is accountable to whom?

   _____

   _____

6. The owner is accountable to whom?

   _____

   _____

7. The contractor is accountable to whom?

   _____

   _____

8. Name some things that can increase the closing cost of a loan.

9. Can architects be held liable for casual statements about the safety of a project?

10. When is it not a good time to ask the architect to do a punch list?

11. Can the contractor deviate from the plans without the architect's approval?

12. Change orders are used by some contractors to do what?

Chapter 11

Schedule of Values and Payment Requests

The language of the signed contract between the owner and contractor is crucial. Also, the understanding of the certificate for payment's application as it relates to the bid's schedule of values is just as important. Why? The certificate for payment determines when and how much the contractor is paid in the progression of the building initiative. Payment to the contractor should always be based upon a percentage of the total work to be completed. Work to be completed is a percentage of the total square footage of the building project or quantity of work to be done. Case in point, if a building has 20 doors to be installed, the installing of 5 doors represent ¼ of work completed. If the contractor's bid price states $5,000.00 for the installation of 20 doors than the certificate for payments should reflect only 25% ($1,250.00) of the total bid price for installing 5 doors. Sometimes a square foot approach determines how much is paid to the contractor and at other times the total days allowed for completion of the project determines how much is paid to the contractor. For example, the contractor is to provide temporary offices, at his or her expense and the job is to be completed in 180 days; each day represents a percentage of the total. If the contractor has only been on the job for 30 days, he has earned appropriately 11% of the total bid price for temporary offices. If an amount is paid to the contractor that exceeds the earned percentage, the contractor is being paid for work not in place.

Contractors use the schedule of values:

1. To justify the bid amount
2. For request of payments
3. To show percentage of completion
4. To track changes to the bid amount
5. For a legal document in case of a dispute
6. For the architect's requirements
7. For the bank's requirements
8. To show a flow of the construction components

Most lending institutions require that contractors present the owner with a schedule of values before approving the loan. However, if you do not require the services of a lender, do not sign a contract without a schedule of values document.

The schedule of values used, in the following illustrations are for the same job.

Illustration 18

Schedule of Values: QKA Construction Company

1	General Conditions	51,072.00
2	Demolition	9,120.00
3	Concrete	
4	Brick Masonry	
5	Metals	
	Trusses	76288.00
6	Carpentry	
	Framing	11,243.82

	Thermal & Moisture Protection	
	Insulation	18,726.78
	Damp proofing & Caulking	3,990.00
	Dryvitt	10,317.00
	Roofing	5,479.98
8	Siding, Soffit, & Gutters	7,514.88
	Doors, Windows & Hardware	
9	Finishes	
	Stud Framing & Drywall	25,793.64
	Acoustical Ceiling	0.00
	Ceramic Tile	7,410.00
	Carpeting & Base	15,427.62
	Painting	16,116.18
	Wallpaper	
10	Specialties	
	Canopy	8,261.58
	Toilet Accessories	3,990.00
11	Equipment	
12	Furnishings	
13	Special Construction	
14	Conveying System	
	Elevator	34,200.00
15	Mechanical	
	Plumbing	10,680.00
	HVAC	15,450.00
16	Electrical	19,850.00
Total		365,866.28

The project was awarded to the contractor in illustration 19. Please compare terminology and cost used. Both companies had the same plans and specifications.

Illustration 19

Schedule of Values: CDP Construction Group

Item Number	Description of Work	Schedule of Value
1	Mobilization	15,000.00
2	Demolition	22,000.00
3	Metal Framing	65,000.00
4	Elevator	32,000.00
5	Interior Walls	18,000.00
6	Drywall	32,000.00
7	Electrical	32,000.00
8	Flooring	12,000.00
9	Doors	11,800.00
10	Trim	6,200.00
11	Plumbing	12,000.00
13	Electrical	18,500.00
14	Mechanical	28,000.00
15	Guttering	4,800.00
16	Interior Repairs	11,000.00
Total	Project will be built according to plans and codes requirements	320,000.00

Even though the architect's specifications are not illustrated, it is easy to see that both contractors didn't schedule all items as presented by the architect. When comparing CDP Construction Company to QKA Construction Company, it is obvious that something is wrong. As an owner, do not consider a bid without a schedule of values. Always compare the schedule of values to the architect's specifications and to the other bidders. In the next illustration, the difference in terminology, multiple items on the same line and the lack of categories of the scope of work is highlighted.

Illustration 20

QKA Construction Company	CDP Construction Group
Has terms of the schedule of values with no dollar amounts for required work	Schedule of values does not reflect work to be done; such as siding, windows, ceramic tile, acoustical ceiling, etc
Does not define electrical and low voltage wiring.	Disguised terms to get funds upfront: mobilization is actual general conditions.
Blank spaces for listed items can be used to charge the owner additional funds. Always insist that the contractor uses the word "included" if the item is included in the bid price. If a term is listed and is not included, the contractor should use the words "not included".	The lack of descriptive work is an indication that the categories have been estimated and not bidden by a subcontractor
Shows more than one item on the same line. This is a method used to hide cost.	The simplicity of the list indicates inexperience or an attempt to manipulate the process.

The Bible teaches that Christians should be sober and vigilant. It is very important that you scrutinize the first and subsequent "certificate for payments". Do not allow the process to intimidate you. The process involves what was bidden according to the schedule of values and what is being requested. If you do not understand, ask questions and do not sign the "certificate for payment" until you are satisfied. The request is based upon a percentage of each line item of work to be completed. Case in point, general conditions and/or mobilization are never 100% until the "certificate for occupancy" is issued.

There are several things that you should look for in the "certificate for payment" as it relates to the schedule of values.

Look for the following:

1. A change of terminology
2. Duplication of descriptions
3. Terminology that excludes the whole
4. Description of work that does not make sense
5. Unreasonable percentage of the total
6. Request for payments for work not completed
7. Payment for materials not on premises
8. Pricing of work that seem too high or low
9. A change in cost

In this example, we shall compare CDP Construction Company "certificate for payment" to the submitted schedule of values. Note that the terms and amounts changed. The "certificate for payment" should have the same original amounts and terminology as the bid's schedule of values presented with the bid unless a change order has been presented and approved by the architect and owner. See illustration 19.

Illustration 21

Certificate for Payment Application

CDP Construction Group

Item	Description	Schedule of Values	Work Previous Application	Completed This Period
1	Quality Control	2,500.00		1,000.00
2	Temporary Facilities	12,500.00		8,000.00
3	Concrete	1,800.00		
4	Elevator Pit	5,500.00		5,500.00
5	Masonry	1,800.00		
6	Interior Metal	23,000.00		10,000.00
7	Exterior Metal	15,000.00		
8	Metal Trusses	25,000.00		
9	Metal Stairwell	5,000.00		
10	Guttering	3,850.00		
11	Demo 1st Floor	14,000.00		12,000.00

12	Demo 2nd Floor	8,000.00		
13	Rough Carpentry	2,200.00		
14	Interior Woodwork	2,200.00		
15	Vapor Retard	2,250.00		
16	Building Insulation	10,500.00		
17	Exterior Insulation	6,800.00		
18	Asphalt Shingles	8,500.00		
19	Sheet Metal Flashing	2,200.00		
20	Joint Sealers	850.00		
21	Metal Door-Frames	11,800.00		5,500.00
22	Finish Hardware	3,200.00		
23	Glass & Glazing	5,900.00		
24	Gypsum Wallboard	2,200.00		8,500.00
25	Acoustical Ceilings	8,400.00		
26	Resilient Flooring	5,800.00		
27	Wall Base	2,200.00		

28	Carpet	7,500.00		
29	Painting	4,800.00		
30	Ceramic Tile	6,800.00		
31	Toilet Partitions	3,800.00		
32	Signage	550.00		
33	Fire Extinguishers	1,200.00		
34	Toilet Accessories	2,200.00		
35	Casework	2,000.00		
36	Elevator	24,000.00		9500.00
37	Ductwork	7,200.00		
38	Plumbing	11,500.00		
39	Heating & Cooling	11,800.00		
40	Control System	700.00		
41	Electrical	24,000.00		
42	Wiring Devices	1,000.00		
43	Fixtures	3,200.00		

If you know what to look for, you can determine from the first "certificate for payment" the contractor's integrity. Some things will show up in the request for payments others will manifest themselves in the attitude of the contractor and his laborers. You can determine if the schedule of values were bidden by subcontractors or if they are in the imagination of the general contractor. You can determine the general contractor's cash flow.

Example:

1. Requesting a large percentage of non-labor items
2. Line items with labor intensity
3. The lack of quantity of materials for immediate building
4. Line items where percentage might be highly subjective
5. Completion of work that is out of sync
6. A request to buy equipment that cannot be installed or stored
7. A request to be paid for non-needed materials
8. A constant scrutinizing of plans for "change order" requests
9. Safety equipment not provided for workers
10. Insufficient tools for laborers
11. Subcontractor's workmanship
12. Requesting funds for trusses, elevators, prefabricated doors, and other large-ticket items rather than owner paying vendors
13. Contractor has selective amnesia
14. A refusal to have completed work inspected

Time and space do allow for a detailed explanation for all of the above. However, there are several factors that indicate cash flow problems.

Indication of Cash Flow Problems:

1. Putting down a finished floor and the ceiling and painting are not complete
2. Workers standing around doing nothing because materials are not on the premises
3. Workers do not have the proper tools to do their work
4. Contractor refusal to have completed work inspected timely. This technique is used to withhold subcontractors' payments for completed work.
5. The contractor telling you every other day the architect missed some details on the plans that require a "change order"
6. Workers complaining about their pay
7. Bill collectors calling on the job
8. Demands to buy materials rather than allowing the owner to pay vendor directly for tax savings
9. Attempts to increase the scope of work beyond plans

In the next illustration, we will look at CDP Construction Company's submitted "schedule of values" as it relates to the "certificate for payment's application" from illustration 19 and 21. The architect's specifications are not listed but are referred to as a matter of fact.

Illustration 22

Comparing Schedule of Values & Application for Payment

Change of Terminology

- Sixteen terms were used in the schedule of values. However forty-three terms were used in the certificate for payment's application. Only four terms in the schedule of values are the same in the certificate for payment's application.

Duplication of Descriptions

- There is one duplication of description of work.

Exclusive Terminology of the Whole

- Elevator pit excludes the shaft, etc.

Descriptive Work That Doesn't Relate to the Architect's Specifications

- Quality control
- Vapor Retard
- Joint Sealers
- Casework
- Exterior Insulation
- Interior Repairs

Unreasonable Percentage of the Total Requested

- The building required twenty-seven doors and frames.
- At the time of request, no frames were hung and the second floor had not been demolished. The

1st floor only required 10 doors and frames. Contractor requested 46.6% of the total line item for payment.

- Contractor requested 100% of elevator pit, yet, the framing for the shaft and walls were not completed.
- Contractor requested 64% of temporary facilities and he had one rental storage pod on the premises. The job was scheduled for 180 days.
- Contractor requested 43% for interior steel; the building had approximately 5,200 square feet and only 1,000 square feet were on the 1st floor. The second floor had not been demolished
- Contractor requested 38.6% for wallboard, yet, the 1st floor was only equal to 19% of the square footage of the project and less than one half of the 1st floor was completed

Request for Work not Completed

- Wallboard
- Interior Steel Walls
- Temporary Facilities
- Elevator
- Doors & Frames

Payment for Materials on Premises

- Gypsum Wallboard
- The contractor didn't have the appropriate quantity of materials on the premises.

Demolition Request

- The project required 1st floor and 2nd floor demolition work.

- Second floor had approximately 4,200 square feet and two roofs to be removed as well as other debris.
- The first floor had less than 800 square feet to be demolished.
- The certificate for payments requested an inappropriate payment.

Pricing of Work

- Pricing of 1st floor demolition is too high.
- Elevator pit is too high for size and depth.
- Metal stairwell too low for plans
- Building insulation too high for design
- Metal frames too high
- Doors were not priced.
- Fire extinguishers too high
- No price for smoke detectors systems

Cost Variations between Schedule of Values and C F P

- Mobilization becomes quality controls and temporary facilities no pricing change
- Demolition is divided with no pricing change.
- Metal framing increased $3,800.00 under the certificate for payment subcategories.
- Doors become metal door frames leaving a zero value for doors
- Elevator becomes elevator pit and elevator, decreasing category $2,500.00
- Drywall becomes gypsum wallboard, decreasing category $10,000.00
- Electrical values decrease $26,500.00.

- Trim becomes interior woodwork, rough-in carpentry and casework increasing category $200.00
- Plumbing decreases $500.00
- Mechanical becomes heating & cooling, duct work and control system decreasing category $8,300.00
- Guttering decreases $950.00
- Interior repairs are lost in the certificate for payment.

Conclusion:

An analysis of CDP Construction Company's submitted schedule of values and the certificate for payment's application reveal the following:

1. The general contractor is inexperienced or has no integrity.
2. He has a serious cash flow problem.
3. He knows how to manipulate the process.
4. The work was not bidden by subcontractors.
5. The general contractor estimated cost.
6. The contractor has no conscience of rights and wrongs.

Using the schedule of values and the "certificate for payment" as an indicator reveals the contractor's character and financial position for your project. **Do not accept a bid from a contractor without schedule of values.** Compare the terminology of the architect's specifications to contractor's terminology. Ask questions about terms you do not understand. Do not allow yourself to be intimidated. Do not depend upon the architect to watch your back. Do not depend upon the codes' officials to watch your back. To some degree they will protect your interest; however, they do not have the time or responsibility to protect you from the full wrath of a dishonesty contractor. They will not and cannot involve themselves in contractual disputes beyond their duties. Therefore, I strongly suggest that the owner has a person whose assignment is to protect the integrity of the job. This person needs to be accessible, visit the job at least three times a day, and have knowledge of the building trade.

Owner's Occupancy

Before you occupy your facility, several things will take place in the final stages. You should have received all of your final inspections for licensed work. Before requesting the Fire Marshal's inspection, the contractor, architect and owner should do a walk-through to make sure everything is to the owner's satisfaction and the project is ready for inspection. Usually, contractor's and architect's final punch lists are developed at this time. However, an experienced contractor will use a punch list throughout the job to keep up with the progression of the project until its completion.

If the architect believes or knows of things that have not been completed according to plans, he may decline to do a punch list with the approval of the owner. This is rare and only occurs when funds are not available to do the work and the uncompleted work is cosmetic and non-structural. Otherwise, the architect will do a final punch list. The punch list and a "Final Completion Checklist" is mailed to the contractor that requires both the owner's and the contractor's signature. Once the work is completed and the form is properly signed, the architect will sign and mail to the contractor a "Certificate of Completion or Substantial Completion." This form initiates the final payment to the contractor less funds held in the "retainage (retaining) account".

Retainage (retaining) funds should not be released to the contractor until the project has been checked for mechanic's liens and the owner is presented a "Certificate of Occupancy" from the agency that issued the building permit. If you borrowed funds from a bank, they will make sure that the project is closed correctly.

Finally, every project deserves a dedicatory program or grand opening. If the project is completed before a scheduled date, you are ready for your dedication program. However, in most instances, the actual date of completion is not a certainty. Therefore, be prepared to request a "Conditional Occupancy". If the structure is a facility that will be viewed and not occupied, the Fire Marshal will usually grant a viewing of the facility without having passed it. Please check with your local Fire Marshal before allowing the public to view a structure that has not passed the Fire Marshal's inspection. In some cases, the owner might be subjected to fines.

NOW YOU CAN SHOUT! IT'S OVER!

Chapter Eleven

Questions for Discussion

1. Name several things that the schedule of values does.

2. The certificate for payment is based upon what factors?

3. Why should the certificate for payment be scrutinized as it relates to the schedule of values?

4. Which characteristics of a contractor can be determined from the certificate for payment?

5. Name several things that reveal cash flow problems in a contractor's certificate for payment.

6. Name several building flaws that reveal a serious cash flow problem?

7. Why isn't it wise to put faith in codes' officials to protect you from

a dishonest contractor?

_____

_____

8. Before you can occupy a newly constructed facility, what needs to take place?

_____

_____

9. When should the Fire Marshal be called to inspect a newly constructed facility?

_____

_____

10. What is a punch list?

_____

_____

11. Before the final payment can be requested, what does the contractor need from the architect?

_____

_____

12. Before the final payment is released, what does the owner need from the contractor?

_____

_____

Chapter 12

Home Improvement Companies

Sometimes the required work does not generate a profit margin that attracts large construction companies but demands skills beyond the average handyman. Any job that is less than $50,000.00 is a step-down for a most licensed general contractor. Home improvement companies primarily fill this void. Some of these companies are unlicensed by the state's contractor board. However, many of them have a local business license. Some of them even advertise as being licensed and bonded. These companies usually have multi building skills. Sometimes, a person who owns and operates a home improvement company is called a jack-of-all-trades. Before hiring a home improvement company, do your "due diligence".

Many of these companies do not have sufficient cash flow to carry a job. Make sure that the company has the capacity to do the work. They will usually give you a written estimate and request a third of the estimated cost as a down payment. In lieu of giving the contractor funds, make checks payable to vendors. Sometimes the contractor will give you a list of materials to buy. I strongly recommend not giving funds for work that is not in place.

It is recommended that a signed contract that protects the owner and contractor be used. As the owner, you need a contract that states what is to be done, the starting and completion date of the job, quality of material, brand names, colors and workmanship's warranty, to name a few. It is always advisable to use the service of a lawyer for contractual language.

Often, owners have budget limitations. However, keep in mind that you get what you pay for. This does not mean: the more something costs the better it is. It does mean that cheap is not always the best. Therefore, make sure that you and the Home Improvement contractor have a clear understanding what is to be done. *Case in point, you hire a person to install ceiling fans. Installing fans requires that some of the ceiling be removed. Upon completion, you notice a hole in your ceiling around the fan's base. The contractor responds, "I was hired to install the fans not repair the ceiling".* A statement instructing the contractor to install, repair ceiling, and paint ceiling with matching paint would be appropriate. Now, to do this would cost more money but it is better than assuming that the contractor will fulfill your expectations.

Electrical and plumbing work may require a licensed person. Make sure that you understand the codes' requirements before hiring unlicensed persons for jobs that require licensed persons. You can call your local codes' office for clarity.

Some home improvement companies or small contractors do not carry insurance. Some small contractors only purchase insurance when they get a job. In any case, the insurance will most likely be insufficient. Therefore, you need to understand the potential liabilities of having people working on your property without sufficient insurance. In my opinion, you need to be protected from bodily injury, medical payments, property damages and workman compensation injuries, to name a few. If the contractor has insurance, request a certificate of insurance from his or her agent. Be sure to get a phone number so you can verify the information and coverage. Be sure to inform the agent about the scope of work in writing or a documented phone call. In other words, tell the agent what the contractor has contracted to do. In some instances, contractors do not reveal the total scope of work to keep their insurance premium low.

If the contractor does not have or refuses to get insurance and a potential loss is highly possible, you can secure the appropriate coverage and negotiate the cost of the project. However, I strongly recommend that homeowners call their insurance agent before starting a major remodeling or renovation project.

Finally, beware of people roaming the neighborhood looking to do work immediately after storms and other natural disasters. Most times these companies will be out of town companies. They will advertise in the local new papers and some will have TV advertisements. Do not sign a contract without a lawyer's advice. **Never sign a blank contract to be completed by the contractor at a later date**. If the contractor has a problem with you taking his contract to your lawyer, you are most likely dealing with a dishonest person. It is better to pay a lawyer $100.00 to read a contract than to have your property tied up in court with a dishonest contractor.

Chapter Twelve

Questions for Discussion

1. What void does a home improvement company fills?

   _____

   _____

2. A home improvement company should have what type of license?

   _____

   _____

3. In lieu of cash to the contractor for work not in place, what can be done?

   _____

   _____

4. Why should a contract be used for a small job?

   _____

   _____

5. Why it is best to have a lawyer read a contract?

   _____

   _____

Appendix 1
A Glossary of Terms

Terminologies used in the glossary are the understanding of the author's knowledge of the building trade. Exceptions are noted by the symbol, www, which indicates the work of Home Building Manual: www.HomeBuildingManual.com

AIA: American Institute of Architects

Appraisal: A valuation of property usually made by a licensed person for mortgage purposes.

Approved Plans: Approved plans are the architectural drawings of a project that have been stamped by every licensed person required by codes.

Architect's Trade-off: Sometimes the architect will admit to an architectural error and solve the problem by getting the owner and contractor to agree to a change in the specifications. Case in point, the specifications call for a particular brand name of carpet. The architect gives the contractor the permission to buy a different brand name of carpet that cost less in hope of off-setting the additional cost to the contractor that was caused by the architect's error. This is called an "architect's trade-off".

As-Is Drawing: Highlighted drawings on the architectural plans indicating changes to size or other structural features by the general contractor

Back Charge: Work performed by one person for another person who had a contractual obligation, In other words, the contractor was under contract to do the work but the owner had it done. Therefore, the owner has a right to bill for the work. In most instances, the contractor will execute a credit "change order" in favor of the owner.

Backfill: The replacement of dirt into previously dug trenches.

Backing: Frame lumber installed between the wall studs to give additional support for drywall or an interior trim-related items, such as handrail brackets, cabinets, and towel bars. In this way, items are screwed and mounted into solid wood rather than into weak drywall that may allow the item to break loose from the wall. Carpet backing holds the pile fabric in place. (www)

Bid Bond: A bond issued by a surety on behalf of a contractor that provides assurance to the recipient of the contractor's bid that, if the bid is accepted, the contractor will execute a contract and provides a performance bond. Under the bond, the surety is obligated to pay the recipient of the bid the difference between the contractor's bid and the bid of the next lowest responsible bidder if the bid is accepted and the contractor fails to execute a contract or to provide a performance bond. (www)

Bid Shopping: A practice used by general contractor to shop prices among subcontractors for specified labor and materials.

Bonded: Funds deposited with an agency that licenses contractors or a fidelity agreement underwritten by an insurance company.

Builder's Risk Insurance: A policy issued to owners to cover the materials of a building project. In some instances, an insurance company will issue a regular policy if the project is 85% complete.

Building Codes: Building codes are specified ordinances of a federal, state or local government that dictates to the construction of buildings and infrastructure.

Certificate of Completion: This is a form that the architect gives to the contractor after all of the requirements of the plans are completed. Sometimes the architect will issue a Substantial of Completion to initiate the contractor's final certificate for payments if the uncompleted work is minor and agreeable with the owner.

Certificate for Payment: This is sometimes called a "draw request". It is a notarized application listing the schedule of values as it relates to work in place. On each application for payments, the contractor bills the owner for work in place until the bid amount is exhausted. Each application list the amount in retainage, change orders' amounts, and total work completed and the remaining work to be completed in dollar amounts. The application has to be signed and approved by the architect before it is presented to the owner for payment.

CO or UO: In some states the term is Certificate of Occupancy. But in Tennessee the term is Use and Occupancy both terms mean the agency that issued the building permit deems that the building is complete according to plans and codes' guidelines and is ready to occupy.

Construction Contract: The construction contract is the contractual agreement that the contractor and owner enter into in order to build the proposed project. There are several types of contracts.

Damp Proofing: This is waterproofing material applied to the exterior of a foundation wall. It varies in colors and usually comes in rolls like fabric.

Discovery: The revelation of unknown factors that increase the financial burden of an obligated person. Case in point, a contractor bids to take off a roof, the roof appears to be asphalt shingles but it has steel cables attached to the trusses. Who is responsible for the additional cost to remove the roof? If the condition could not be known by the contractor by sight or access to the attic, and the plans are ambiguous, and the contract doesn't stipulates discovery responsibilities, the owner will most likely end up paying for the additional cost either by a "change order" or an "architect's trade-off".

Draftsmen: Draftsmen are persons who draw structural plans for architects. In some instances, they take the measurements and initiate a scale drawing.

Drywall (or Gypsum Wallboard (GWB), Sheet rock or Plasterboard): Wallboard or gypsum- A manufactured panel made out of gypsum plaster and encased in a thin cardboard, usually 1/2" thick and 4' x 8' or 4' x 12' in size. The panels are nailed or screwed onto the framing and the joints are taped and covered with a 'joint compound'. 'Green board' type drywall has a greater resistance to moisture than regular (white) plasterboard and is used in bathrooms and other "wet areas". (www.)

Electrical Rough: Work performed by the Electrical Contractor after the plumber and heating contractor complete their phase of work. Normally all electrical wires and outlets, switches, and fixture boxes are installed before insulation. (www)

Final Completion Checklist: This is a form given to the owner and contractor. It is a list of things that need to be done before the architect will sign a Certificate of Completion.

Fire-Resistive or Fire Rated: Applies to materials that are not combustible in the temperatures of ordinary fires and will withstand such fires for at least 1 hour. Drywall used in the garage and party walls are to be fire rated, 5/8", Type X
(www.)

GF C I or G F I: Ground Fault Circuit Interrupter an ultra- sensitive plug designed to shut off all electric current. Used in bathrooms, kitchens, exterior waterproof outlets, garage outlets, and "wet areas". Has a small reset button on the plug. (www.)

General Contractor: A general contractor is a person or entity that has the capacity and license to enter into a contractual relationship to build a project for another.

Giving Units: This term denotes the number of persons in an organization that are over a specified age that earn a separate income. It is used by banks as one of its means for qualifying churches for loans.

Heating Load: This is a term that is used by the building trade as an indicator of the flow of heat to maintain a building at a specified temperature.

Historical Agencies: Agencies that have the responsibility for identifying and preserving unique aged structures.

H V A C: An abbreviation for Heat, Ventilation, and Air Conditioning. (www.)

HVAC Balance Report: The measurement of heating and cooling velocity of the heating and cooling unit as it flows to each area of a building

Insulation: Any material high in resistance to heat transmission that, when placed in the walls, ceiling, or floors of a structure, will reduce the rate of heat flow. (www.)

Manufacturer's specifications: The written installation and/or maintenance instructions which are developed by the manufacturer of a product and which may have to be followed in order to maintain the product warrantee. (www.)

Mechanic's lien: A lien on real property, created by statue in many states, in favor of persons supplying labor or materials for a building or structure, for the value of labor or materials supplied by them. In some jurisdictions, a mechanic lien also exists for the value of professional services. Clear title to the property cannot be obtained until the claim for the labor, materials, or professional services is settled. Timely filing is essential to support the encumbrance, and prescribed filing dates vary by jurisdiction. (www.)

Millwork: Generally, all building materials made of finished wood and manufactured in millwork plants, include all doors, window and door frames, blinds, mantels, panel work, stairway components (balusters, rail, etc.), moldings, and interior trim. Does not include flooring, ceiling, or siding. (www.)

Performance Bond: This is a bond that is issued by an insurance company on the behalf of its insurer that guarantees work to be performed by a contractor. If the contractor does not live up to the terms of the contractual agreement, the owner receives specified funds to complete the job.

Permit-Ready Plans: Plans given to the owner by the architect that has been reviewed by codes with a permit to build. If possible, always request permit-ready plans.

Punch List: A list of things that need to be done to move a building project forward or things that have not been completed according to the plans. Usually, it is a negative when it used before completion of the project.

Retaining Account: It is spelled in the industry -- retainage". This account is used to deposit 10% or a specified percentage of each certificate for payments paid to the contractor until the project is completed and the owner receives a Use and Occupancy permit.

Scope of Work: The architectural drawings denote what work is needed on the project. This is called the scope of work. Be careful of contractors who attempt to get you to go beyond the scope of work for their profit. Both general contractors and subcontractors use this technique to get additional funds out of a project.

Specifications: These are written instructions that accommodate the architect's plans.

Stop Order: This is a written notice given to the contractor to cease all work. It can be issued by the owner or agencies having jurisdiction over the building project. The reason for the order may vary depending upon who issues it.

Stud: This term is used to denote a vertical beam that makes contact with two horizontal beams, one beneath and the other above. It can be wood or steel.

Sub-flooring: This is a material, usually plywood or a like-material, which is nailed to the floor joist.

Threshold: The bottom metal or wood plate of an exterior door frame. Generally, it is adjustable to keep a tight fit with the door slab. (www.)

Top Heavy Contract: This is a contract whereby the general contractor places a large percentage of his or her mark-up in non-labor and other categories of the schedule of values to get immediate funds out of the contract. Case in point, a contractor may overcharge the owner for general conditions, demolition, temporary offices, and others start-up costs within the contract. Contractors that use this approach are to be watched carefully.

UL (Underwriters' Laboratories): An independent testing agency that checks electrical devices and other components for possible safety hazards. (www.)

Underlay Materials: A ¼" material placed over the sub floor plywood sheeting and under finish coverings, such as vinyl flooring, to provide a smooth, even surface. Also a secondary roofing layer that is waterproof, or water-resistant, installed on the roof deck and beneath shingles or other roof-finishing layer. (www.)

Valley: The "V" shaped area of a roof where two sloping roofs meet. Water drains off the roof at the valleys.

Valley flashing: Sheet metal that lies in the "V" area of a roof valley.

Wafer board: A manufactured wood panel made out of 1"- 2" wood chips and glue. Often used as a substitute for plywood in the exterior wall and roof sheathing. (www.)

Warranty: In construction, there are two general types of warranties. One is provided by the manufacturer of a product such as roofing material or equipment. The second is a warranty for the labor. For example, a roofing contract may include a 20-year material warranty and a 1-year labor warranty. Many new homebuilders provide a one-year labor warranty. Any major issue found during the first year should be communicated to the builder immediately.

Zoning: Zoning is a term that denotes statues and ordinances that are passed by the elected officials of a county or municipality that determines how property can be used and developed.

Appendix 2
Funding Possibilities

The type of financing used to fund a project is crucial. Listed here are available sources of funding.

Commercial Banks

Most churches use banks. The bank is a familiar lender and presents the least threat of being a predator lender. The bank will loan an amount of funds that the client is able to debit service based upon the, LTV, Loan to Value of the completed project.

The bank will require three years of financial records, bank statements, church directory, giving units, resume of pastor, history and age of the church, and credit and character references.

The bank interest rates are quoted in percentage over prime and the loan period is usually less than thirty years. A bank loan for building purposes has two components, construction and permanent. While the project is under construction the borrower pays the lender a fixed interest rate on the funds as used. At the completion of the project, the loan is converted to a permanent loan and principal and interest payments are made to the lender in one note.

Church Bonds

In recent years, churches, (because of doctrine, "owe no man anything but love" and for members' participation in the reaping of the church's financial blessings), use church bonds to finance their building initiatives. Church bonds are securities.

Church bonds require basely the same requirements as the bank but it involves the security and exchange regulations of the issuance state. Also, it requires the services of a myriad of licensed professional assistance. It is a safe investment and the investor's funds are secured by the project.

Church bonds are issued in denominations and for a specified period with a fix rate. Using church bonds, allows the church the opportunity to amortize the repayment of the investor's funds usually at an amount less than paying a monthly bank note. (Also, it allows church members the opportunity to receive the interest that otherwise would be paid to the bank.) Also, the church is not penalized for the usage of funds during the construction of the project. The church needs to weigh the fees to issue the bonds versus the interest charged by the bank and its fees.

Church bonds are usually issued at a rate higher than T-Bills and Government Savings Bonds to attract investors and they are sold to the general public.

Venture Capital

This type of funding can be predatory in nature. It is used mostly by start-up businesses that have no capital but have a highly marketable product. The usages of these funds have no set interest rate but it is always higher than the bank. Usually the venture capitalist seeks to owe a percentage of the business. In the case of a church, it may have prime property that attracts the interest of a venture capitalist.

Investment Capital

At any given time, there are persons that have more funds than are required for personal and pleasurable needs. Sometimes a person or a company looks to invest their funds for tax write-offs, ideological reasons, and for a safe return above market values.

If the church packages its offering with care and due diligence, funds are available. However, some investors prefer not to have their funds secured by the church's sanctuary. Interest rates and loan periods are negotiable. Therefore, the church needs to have other properties to secure the investment, such as rental properties.

Self Finance

There was a time when most churches did not meet the bank's criteria for loans. During this time, members sold fish and chicken dinners to finance the building of the church. In other words, they would build as they had funds. Usually, the church would raise funds for the foundation, walls, truss, and roof and so forth until the building was completed. Members and volunteer labor did the work. Even though this was a slow process, upon completion the building was paid for.

However, due to codes' requirements for labor and building, it is difficult to use this technique. People do not have the time or refuse to give the time that made this concept workable. Most churches have graduated from fish and chicken dinners. The cost of materials is so unstable that a $25,000.00 project could end up costing $50,000.00-plus upon completion.

For projects less than $25,000.00, this concept is still used by some small congregations. However, if a church has members that have the capacity to donate large sums of funds, this is a workable approach for larger projects.

Church Mortgage Certificates

This concept is a hybrid of the church bonds, commercial bank, and investment capitalists. The approach is sound, legal and secures the investor's funds and allows the church the opportunity to determine its interest rate, while amortizing its indebtedness. If a church has members that understand the investment market and have access to discretionary funds, this concept offers the church the best funding opportunity.

For more information about this concept, write the author at 905 South Douglas Avenue, Nashville, Tennessee 37204.

Appendix 3
States' Web Pages

Every state has a web page that gives the essentials for contractor's requirements. In addition, the state office will be able to put you in contact will local agencies in your particular area. Every state of the United States is listed.

Each state has a different format for presenting its information to the public. It is the author's intent to make known to its readers a compilation of shared information from the public domain.

The State of Alabama

   http://www.statelocalgov.net/state-al.cfm

The State of Alaska

   http://www.state.ak.us/

The State of Arizona

   http://www.statelocalgov.net/state-al.cfm

The State of Arkansas

   http://www.state.ar.us/

The State of California

   http://www.cbs.state.or.us/external/bcd/

The State of Colorado

   http://www.colorado.gov/

The State of Connecticut

> http://www.ct.gov/

The State of Delaware

> http://delaware.gov/

The State of Florida

> http://www.myflorida.com/

The State of Georgia

> http://www.georgia.gov/

The State of Hawaii

> http://www.hawaii.gov/portal/

The State of Idaho

> http://www.state.id.us/

The State of Illinois

> http://www.illinois.gov/

The State of Indiana

> http://www.state.in.us/

The State of Iowa

> http://www.iowa.gov/state/main/index.html

The State of Kansas

> http://www.accesskansas.org/

The State of Kentucky

> http://kentucky.gov/

The State of Louisiana

> http://www.louisiana.gov/wps/portal/

The State of Maine

> http://www.state.me.us/

The State of Maryland

> http://maryland.gov

The State of Massachusetts

> http://www.mass.gov/portal

The State of Michigan

> http://www.michigan.gov/

The State of Minnesota

> http://www.state.mn.us

The State of Mississippi

> http://www.state.ms.us

The State of Missouri

> http://www.state.mo.us

The State of Montana

> http://www.mt.gov/

The State of Nebraska

> http://www.nebraska.gov/index.phtml

The State of Nevada

> http://www.nv.gov/

The State of New Hampshire

> http://www.state.nh.us/

The State of New Jersey

> http://www.state.nj.us/

The State of New Mexico

> http://www.state.nm.us/

The State of New York

> http://www.state.ny.us/

The State of North Carolina

> http://www.sips.state.nc.us/

The State of North Dakota

    http://discovernd.com/

The State of Ohio

    http://ohio.gov/

The State of Oklahoma

    http://www.ok.gov/

The State of Oregon

    http://www.oregon.gov/

The State of Pennsylvania

    http://www.state.pa.us/

The State of Rhode Island

    http://www.state.ri.us/

The State of South Carolina

    http://www.myscgov.com

The State of South Dakota

    http://www.state.sd.us/

The State of Tennessee

    http://www.state.tn.us/commerce/

    http://www.nashville.gov/codes/index.html

The State of Texas

> http://www.state.tx.us/

The State of Utah

> http://www.utah.gov/

The State of Vermont

> http://vermont.gov/

The State of Virginia

> http://legis.state.va.us

The State of Washington

> http://access.wa.gov/

The State of West Virginia

> http://www.wv.gov/

The State of Wisconsin

> http://www.wisconsin.gov

The State of Wyoming

> http://wyoming.gov

Mapp, Esther

Hunter Ave. Baptist Church